Proverbs Write

일러두기

1. 본서는 NIV®(New International version)를 채택하여 필사할 수 있도록 한글(개역개정)과 함께 구성했습니다.

2. 한글 성경은 (재)대한성서공회가 발행한 『성경전서 개역개정판』을 사용하였습니다.

3. '영어성경 잠언.쓰다'는 만년필 사용이 가능한 친환경 종이를 사용하였습니다.

Pr.

NIV®

Proverbs Write
영어성경 잠언.쓰다

에이프릴지저스

잠언 말씀

하나님께 속한 백성으로 살아 갈때에, 영적으로 또 도덕적으로 세상속에서 꼭 지녀야 할 규칙을 잘 지키고 그로인해 하나님께서 기뻐하실 삶을 살게 하기 위하여 기록되었습니다.

잠언은 솔로몬이 하나님께서 주신 지혜를 기록하고 있는데 이 놀라운 지혜들은 현실을 살아가는 우리에게도 반드시 적용되어 경험하기를 이야기하고 있습니다. 또한 이 모든 참된 지혜는 여호와를 온전히 경외할 때 얻을 수 있다는 것을 계속하여 진술하고 있습니다. 꼭 경험해야 할 놀라운 지혜로 가득한 잠언을, 영어 필사를 통해 온전히 나의 지혜로 만드는 경험을 하시길 바랍니다.

우리 모두 하나님의 말씀대로 살며 축복의 통로가 되는 그리스도인이 되기를 소망합니다.

잠언의 구성 | 31장 915절

1-9장	솔로몬의 잠언
10장-22:16	솔로몬의 잠언
22:17-24장	지혜자의 잠언
25-29장	히스기야왕 신하들이 편집한 솔로몬의 잠언
30-31장	아굴과 르무엘의 잠언

1. 필사를 시작하기 전에 기도하세요.
   주기도문! 사도신경으로 신앙고백을 하며 마음가짐을 다져요.

2. 좌측의 성경 말씀을 천천히 한자 한자 정성껏 쓰면서 큰소리로 읽으세요. 눈, 입, 귀 세 감각이 영어를 접하고 익히게 됩니다. 영어 성경은 하나님 말씀과 영어를 동시에 배울 수 있어요. 한글과는 또다른 은혜가 부어질 것입니다.

3. 읽고, 필사한 말씀을 묵상하세요.
   필사한 내용을 묵상하며 오늘 나에게 주신 말씀을 삶에 적용해 보세요.

4. 필사 후 역사하실 하나님을 기대하며 기도로 마무리 합니다.

왜 모눈(그리드) 인가?

간격이 정해진 줄노트는 생각의 폭이 줄안에 갇힐수 있으므로 생각 확장이 제한됩니다. 공간 활용에 자유로운 모눈(grid)노트로 말씀에만 집중하며 나의 글씨 크기대로 자유롭게 필사하세요.
남는 여유 공간에는 주신 말씀 또는 암송하고 싶은 말씀을 반복해서 써보세요.

필사라는 가장 적극적인 성경읽기를 통해, 말씀이 살아 움직임을 느끼고 삶의 변화까지 선물 받는 놀라운 필사의 경험을 스스로에게 선물하기를 바랍니다.

Contents

가장 적극적인 성경읽기는 필사입니다 !

WRITER :

START DATE :

COMPLETE DATE :

The Lord's Prayer

Our Father in heaven,
hallowed be your name,
your kingdom come, your will be done
on earth as it is in heaven.
Give us today our daily bread.
Forgive us our debts,
as we also have forgiven our debtors.
And lead us not into temptation,
but deliver us from the evil one.
(For yours is the kingdom and the power,
and the glory, forever, Amen.)

Matthew 6:9-13

The Lord's Prayer

The Apostles' creed

I believe in God the Father Almighty,
maker of heaven and earth;
And in Jesus Christ, his only Son our Lord:
who was conceived by the Holy Spirit, born of the Virgin Mary,
suffered under Pontius Pilate, was crucified, dead, and buried;
he descended into hell,
the third day he rose again from the dead;
he ascend into heaven,
and sitteth on the right hand of God the Father Almighty;
from thence he shall come to judge the quick and the dead.
I believe in the Holy Spirit, the holy universal church,
the communion of saints,
the forgiveness of sins,
the resurrection of the boby,
and the life everlasting. Amen.

The Apostles' creed

미리보는 어휘

1장

embrace 깨닫다
exhortation 권고
riddle 수수께끼
swift 빠른
waylay 숨어 기다리다
calamity 재앙
complacency 자기만족
distress 고민, 고통
heed 마음에 두다
mockery 조롱
overtake 덮치다
overwhelm 압도하다
rebuke 책망
spurn 경멸하다
waywardness 고집
whirlwind 회오리바람
sweep over : 엄습하다
be at ease : 안심하다

2장

blameless 흠없는
scheme 음모, 계획
spurn 경멸하다
waywardness 고집
whirlwind 회오리바람
adulteress 음녀
covenant 언약
crooked 구부러진
devious 사악한
perverseness 사악함
prosperity 번영
seductive 유혹하는
wayward 고집스러운
apply...to~ : ~에…를 쏟다, 기울이다
be cut off from...: …로부터 끊어지다

3장

shun 피하다, 멀리하다
prosperity 번영
nourishment 자양분
prolong 연장하다
vat 큰통
accuse 고발하다
curse 저주
detest 혐오하다
discernment 분별력
mock 조롱하다
overtake 압도하다
resent 분개하다
perverse 괴팍한
resent 분개하다
snare 덫으로 잡다
inherit 상속하다, 물려받다
plot against 음모를 꾸미다
brim over with ... : …으로 차 넘치다

4장

embrace 받아들이다

esteem 존중하다

exalt 높이다

forsake 저버리다

garland 화환

gleam 미광

hamper 방해하다

slumber 수면, 잠

splendor 광채

stumble 넘어지다

swerve 벗어나다, 어긋나다

tender 연약한

corrupt 부정한, 사악한

wellspring 원천

perversity 사악함

swerve 벗어나다, 어긋나다

swerve from... : …에게 벗어나다

put away : 피하다, 물리치다

5장

adultery 간음, 부정

cistern 저수지

correction 징계

crooked 구부러진, 굴곡된

cruel 잔인한

discretion 분별

double-edged 쌍날의

groan 신음하다

spurn 거절하다

utter 전적인

come to the brink of ... : …하기 직전의 순간에 이르다

in full view of ... : …가 다 보는 곳에

Purpose and Theme

1 The proverbs of Solomon son of David, king of Israel:

2 for gaining wisdom and instruction; for understanding words of insight;

3 for receiving instruction in prudent behavior, doing what is right and just and fair;

4 for giving prudence to those who are simple, knowledge and discretion to the young—

5 let the wise listen and add to their learning, and let the discerning get guidance

6 for understanding proverbs and parables, the sayings and riddles of the wise.

7 The fear of the Lord is the beginning of knowledge, but fools despise wisdom and instruction.

Prologue: Exhortations to Embrace Wisdom

Warning Against the Invitation of Sinful Men

8 Listen, my son, to your father's instruction and do not forsake your mother's teaching.

9 They are a garland to grace your head and a chain to adorn your neck.

10 My son, if sinful men entice you, do not give in to them.

1 다윗의 아들 이스라엘 왕 솔로몬의 잠언이라 2 이는 지혜와 훈계를 알게 하며 명철의 말씀을 깨닫게 하며 3 지혜롭게, 공의롭게, 정의롭게, 정직하게 행할 일에 대하여 훈계를 받게 하며 4 어리석은 자를 슬기롭게 하며 젊은 자에게 지식과 근신함을 주기 위한 것이니 5 지혜 있는 자는 듣고 학식이 더할 것이요 명철한 자는 지략을 얻을 것이라 6 잠언과 비유와 지혜 있는 자의 말과 그 오묘한 말을 깨달으리라 7 여호와를 경외하는 것이 지식의 근본이거늘 미련한 자는 지혜와 훈계를 멸시하느니라 8 내 아들아 네 아비의 훈계를 들으며 네 어미의 법을 떠나지 말라 9 이는 네 머리의 아름다운 관이요 네 목의 금 사슬이니라 10 내 아들아 악한 자가 너를 꾈지라도 따르지 말라

11 If they say, "Come along with us; let's lie in wait for innocent blood, let's ambush some harmless soul;

12 let's swallow them alive, like the grave, and whole, like those who go down to the pit;

13 we will get all sorts of valuable things and fill our houses with plunder;

14 cast lots with us; we will all share the loot"—

15 my son, do not go along with them, do not set foot on their paths;

16 for their feet rush into evil, they are swift to shed blood.

17 How useless to spread a net where every bird can see it!

18 These men lie in wait for their own blood; they ambush only themselves!

19 Such are the paths of all who go after ill-gotten gain; it takes away the life of those who get it.

Wisdom's Rebuke

20 Out in the open wisdom calls aloud, she raises her voice in the public square;

21 on top of the wall she cries out, at the city gate she makes her speech:

22 "How long will you who are simple love your simple ways? How long will mockers delight in mockery and fools hate knowledge?

11 그들이 네게 말하기를 우리와 함께 가자 우리가 가만히 엎드렸다가 사람의 피를 흘리자 죄 없는 자를 까닭 없이 숨어 기다리다가 12 스올 같이 그들을 산 채로 삼키며 무덤에 내려가는 자들 같이 통으로 삼키자 13 우리가 온갖 보화를 얻으며 빼앗은 것으로 우리 집을 채우리니 14 너는 우리와 함께 제비를 뽑고 우리가 함께 전대 하나만 두자 할지라도 15 내 아들아 그들과 함께 길에 다니지 말라 네 발을 금하여 그 길을 밟지 말라 16 대저 그 발은 악으로 달려가며 피를 흘리는 데 빠름이니라 17 새가 보는 데서 그물을 치면 헛일이겠거늘 18 그들이 가만히 엎드림은 자기의 피를 흘릴 뿐이요 숨어 기다림은 자기의 생명을 해할 뿐이니 19 이익을 탐하는 모든 자의 길은 다 이러하여 자기의 생명을 잃게 하느니라 20 지혜가 길거리에서 부르며 광장에서 소리를 높이며 21 시끄러운 길목에서 소리를 지르며 성문 어귀와 성중에서 그 소리를 발하여 이르되 22 너희 어리석은 자들은 어리석음을 좋아하며 거만한 자들은 거만을 기뻐하며 미련한 자들은 지식을 미워하니 어느 때까지 하겠느냐

23 Repent at my rebuke! Then I will pour out my thoughts to you, I will make known to you my teachings.

24 But since you refuse to listen when I call and no one pays attention when I stretch out my hand,

25 since you disregard all my advice and do not accept my rebuke,

26 I in turn will laugh when disaster strikes you; I will mock when calamity overtakes you—

27 when calamity overtakes you like a storm, when disaster sweeps over you like a whirlwind, when distress and trouble overwhelm you.

28 "Then they will call to me but I will not answer; they will look for me but will not find me,

29 since they hated knowledge and did not choose to fear the Lord.

30 Since they would not accept my advice and spurned my rebuke,

31 they will eat the fruit of their ways and be filled with the fruit of their schemes.

32 For the waywardness of the simple will kill them, and the complacency of fools will destroy them;

33 but whoever listens to me will live in safety and be at ease, without fear of harm."

23 나의 책망을 듣고 돌이키라 보라 내가 나의 영을 너희에게 부어 주며 내 말을 너희에게 보이리라 24 내가 불렀으나 너희가 듣기 싫어하였고 내가 손을 폈으나 돌아보는 자가 없었고 25 도리어 나의 모든 교훈을 멸시하며 나의 책망을 받지 아니하였은즉 26 너희가 재앙을 만날 때에 내가 웃을 것이며 너희에게 두려움이 임할 때에 내가 비웃으리라 27 너희의 두려움이 광풍 같이 임하겠고 너희의 재앙이 폭풍 같이 이르겠고 너희에게 근심과 슬픔이 임하리니 28 그 때에 너희가 나를 부르리라 그래도 내가 대답하지 아니하겠고 부지런히 나를 찾으리라 그래도 나를 만나지 못하리니 29 대저 너희가 지식을 미워하며 여호와 경외하기를 즐거워하지 아니하며 30 나의 교훈을 받지 아니하고 나의 모든 책망을 업신여겼음이니라 31 그러므로 자기 행위의 열매를 먹으며 자기 꾀에 배부르리라 32 어리석은 자의 퇴보는 자기를 죽이며 미련한 자의 안일은 자기를 멸망시키려니와 33 오직 내 말을 듣는 자는 평안히 살며 재앙의 두려움이 없이 안전하리라

Moral Benefits of Wisdom

1 My son, if you accept my words and store up my commands within you,

2 turning your ear to wisdom and applying your heart to understanding—

3 indeed, if you call out for insight and cry aloud for understanding,

4 and if you look for it as for silver and search for it as for hidden treasure,

5 then you will understand the fear of the Lord and find the knowledge of God.

6 For the Lord gives wisdom; from his mouth come knowledge and understanding.

7 He holds success in store for the upright, he is a shield to those whose walk is blameless,

8 for he guards the course of the just and protects the way of his faithful ones.

9 Then you will understand what is right and just and fair—every good path.

10 For wisdom will enter your heart, and knowledge will be pleasant to your soul.

1 내 아들아 네가 만일 나의 말을 받으며 나의 계명을 네게 간직하며 2 네 귀를 지혜에 기울이며 네 마음을 명철에 두며 3 지식을 불러 구하며 명철을 얻으려고 소리를 높이며 4 은을 구하는 것 같이 그것을 구하며 감추어진 보배를 찾는 것 같이 그것을 찾으면 5 여호와 경외하기를 깨달으며 하나님을 알게 되리니 6 대저 여호와는 지혜를 주시며 지식과 명철을 그 입에서 내심이며 7 그는 정직한 자를 위하여 완전한 지혜를 예비하시며 행실이 온전한 자에게 방패가 되시나니 8 대저 그는 정의의 길을 보호하시며 그의 성도들의 길을 보전하려 하심이니라 9 그런즉 네가 공의와 정의와 정직 곧 모든 선한 길을 깨달을 것이라 10 곧 지혜가 네 마음에 들어가며 지식이 네 영혼을 즐겁게 할 것이요

11 Discretion will protect you, and understanding will guard you.

12 Wisdom will save you from the ways of wicked men, from men whose words are perverse,

13 who leave the straight paths to walk in dark ways,

14 who delight in doing wrong and rejoice in the perverseness of evil,

15 whose paths are crooked and who are devious in their ways.

16 Wisdom will save you also from the adulterous woman, from the wayward woman with her seductive words,

17 who has left the partner of her youth and ignored the covenant she made before God.

18 Surely her house leads down to death and her paths to the spirits of the dead.

19 None who go to her return or attain the paths of life.

20 Thus you will walk in the ways of the good and keep to the paths of the righteous.

21 For the upright will live in the land, and the blameless will remain in it;

22 but the wicked will be cut off from the land, and the unfaithful will be torn from it.

11 근신이 너를 지키며 명철이 너를 보호하여 12 악한 자의 길과 패역을 말하는 자에게서 건져 내리라 13 이 무리는 정직한 길을 떠나 어두운 길로 행하며 14 행악하기를 기뻐하며 악인의 패역을 즐거워하나니 15 그 길은 구부러지고 그 행위는 패역하니라 16 지혜가 또 너를 음녀에게서, 말로 호리는 이방 계집에게서 구원하리니 17 그는 젊은 시절의 짝을 버리며 그의 하나님의 언약을 잊어버린 자라 18 그의 집은 사망으로, 그의 길은 스올로 기울어졌나니 19 누구든지 그에게로 가는 자는 돌아오지 못하며 또 생명 길을 얻지 못하느니라 20 지혜가 너를 선한 자의 길로 행하게 하며 또 의인의 길을 지키게 하리니 21 대저 정직한 자는 땅에 거하며 완전한 자는 땅에 남아 있으리라 22 그러나 악인은 땅에서 끊어지겠고 간사한 자는 땅에서 뽑히리라

Wisdom Bestows Well-Being

1   My son, do not forget my teaching, but keep my commands in your heart,

2   for they will prolong your life many years and bring you peace and prosperity.

3   Let love and faithfulness never leave you; bind them around your neck, write them on the tablet of your heart.

4   Then you will win favor and a good name in the sight of God and man.

5   Trust in the LORD with all your heart and lean not on your own understanding;

6   in all your ways submit to him, and he will make your paths straight.

7   Do not be wise in your own eyes; fear the LORD and shun evil.

8   This will bring health to your body and nourishment to your bones.

9   Honor the LORD with your wealth, with the firstfruits of all your crops;

10   then your barns will be filled to overflowing, and your vats will brim over with new wine.

11   My son, do not despise the Lord's discipline, and do not resent his rebuke,

1 내 아들아 나의 법을 잊어버리지 말고 네 마음으로 나의 명령을 지키라 2 그리하면 그것이 네가 장수하여 많은 해를 누리게 하며 평강을 더하게 하리라 3 인자와 진리가 네게서 떠나지 말게 하고 그것을 네 목에 매며 네 마음판에 새기라 4 그리하면 네가 하나님 과 사람 앞에서 은총과 귀중히 여김을 받으리라 5 너는 마음을 다하여 여호와를 신뢰하고 네 명철을 의지하지 말라 6 너는 범사에 그를 인정하라 그리하면 네 길을 지도하시리라 7 스스로 지혜롭게 여기지 말지어다 여호와를 경외하며 악을 떠날지어다 8 이것 이 네 몸에 양약이 되어 네 골수를 윤택하게 하리라 9 네 재물과 네 소산물의 처음 익은 열매로 여호와를 공경하라 10 그리하면 네 창고가 가득히 차고 네 포도즙 틀에 새 포도즙이 넘치리라 11 내 아들아 여호와의 징계를 경히 여기지 말라 그 꾸지람을 싫어하지 말라

12 because the LORD disciplines those he loves, as a father the son he delights in.

13 Blessed are those who find wisdom, those who gain understanding,

14 for she is more profitable than silver and yields better returns than gold.

15 She is more precious than rubies; nothing you desire can compare with her.

16 Long life is in her right hand; in her left hand are riches and honor.

17 Her ways are pleasant ways, and all her paths are peace.

18 She is a tree of life to those who take hold of her; those who hold her fast will be blessed.

19 By wisdom the Lord laid the earth's foundations, by understanding he set the heavens in place;

20 by his knowledge the watery depths were divided, and the clouds let drop the dew.

21 My son, do not let wisdom and understanding out of your sight, preserve sound judgment and discretion;

22 they will be life for you, an ornament to grace your neck.

23 Then you will go on your way in safety, and your foot will not stumble.

12 대저 여호와께서 그 사랑하시는 자를 징계하시기를 마치 아비가 그 기뻐하는 아들을 징계함 같이 하시느니라 13 지혜를 얻은 자와 명철을 얻은 자는 복이 있나니 14 이는 지혜를 얻는 것이 은을 얻는 것보다 낫고 그 이익이 정금보다 나음이니라 15 지혜는 진주보다 귀하니 네가 사모하는 모든 것으로도 이에 비교할 수 없도다 16 그의 오른손에는 장수가 있고 그의 왼손에는 부귀가 있나니 17 그 길은 즐거운 길이요 그의 지름길은 다 평강이니라 18 지혜는 그 얻은 자에게 생명 나무라 지혜를 가진 자는 복되도다 19 여호와께서는 지혜로 땅에 터를 놓으셨으며 명철로 하늘을 견고히 세우셨고 20 그의 지식으로 깊은 바다를 갈라지게 하셨으며 공중에서 이슬이 내리게 하셨느니라 21 내 아들아 완전한 지혜와 근신을 지키고 이것들이 네 눈 앞에서 떠나지 말게 하라 22 그리하면 그것이 네 영혼의 생명이 되며 네 목에 장식이 되리니 23 네가 네 길을 평안히 행하겠고 네 발이 거치지 아니하겠으며

24 when you lie down, you will not be afraid; when you lie down, your sleep will be sweet.

25 Have no fear of sudden disaster or of the ruin that overtakes the wicked,

26 for the Lord will be at your side and will keep your foot from being snared.

27 Do not withhold good from those to whom it is due, when it is in your power to act.

28 Do not say to your neighbor, "Come back tomorrow and I'll give it to you"— when you already have it with you.

29 Do not plot harm against your neighbor, who lives trustfully near you.

30 Do not accuse anyone for no reason — when they have done you no harm.

31 Do not envy the violent or choose any of their ways.

32 For the Lord detests the perverse but takes the upright into his confidence.

33 The LORD's curse is on the house of the wicked, but he blesses the home of the righteous.

34 He mocks proud mockers but shows favor to the humble and oppressed.

35 The wise inherit honor, but fools get only shame.

24 네가 누울 때에 두려워하지 아니하겠고 네가 누운즉 네 잠이 달리로다 25 너는 갑작스러운 두려움도 악인에게 닥치는 멸망도 두려워하지 말라 26 대저 여호와는 네가 의지할 이시니라 네 발을 지켜 걸리지 않게 하시리라 27 네 손이 선을 베풀 힘이 있거든 마땅히 받을 자에게 베풀기를 아끼지 말며 28 네게 있거든 이웃에게 이르기를 갔다가 다시 오라 내일 주겠노라 하지 말며 29 네 이웃이 네 곁에서 평안히 살거든 그를 해하려고 꾀하지 말며 30 사람이 네게 악을 행하지 아니하였거든 까닭 없이 더불어 다투지 말며 31 포학한 자를 부러워하지 말며 그의 어떤 행위도 따르지 말라 32 대저 패역한 자는 여호와께서 미워하시나 정직한 자에게는 그의 교통하심이 있으며 33 악인의 집에는 여호와의 저주가 있거니와 의인의 집에는 복이 있느니라 34 진실로 그는 거만한 자를 비웃으시며 겸손한 자에게 은혜를 베푸시나니 35 지혜로운 자는 영광을 기업으로 받거니와 미련한 자의 영달함은 수치가 되느니라

Get Wisdom at Any Cost

1 Listen, my sons, to a father's instruction; pay attention and gain understanding.

2 I give you sound learning, so do not forsake my teaching.

3 For I too was a son to my father, still tender, and cherished by my mother.

4 Then he taught me, and he said to me, "Take hold of my words with all your heart; keep my commands, and you will live.

5 Get wisdom, get understanding; do not forget my words or turn away from them.

6 Do not forsake wisdom, and she will protect you; love her, and she will watch over you.

7 The beginning of wisdom is this: Get wisdom. Though it cost all you have, get understanding.

8 Cherish her, and she will exalt you; embrace her, and she will honor you.

9 She will give you a garland to grace your head and present you with a glorious crown."

10 Listen, my son, accept what I say, and the years of your life will be many.

1 아들들아 아비의 훈계를 들으며 명철을 얻기에 주의하라 2 내가 선한 도리를 너희에게 전하노니 내 법을 떠나지 말라 3 나도 내 아버지에게 아들이었으며 내 어머니 보기에 유약한 외아들이었노라 4 아버지가 내게 가르쳐 이르기를 내 말을 네 마음에 두라 내 명령을 지키라 그리하면 살리라 5 지혜를 얻으며 명철을 얻으라 내 입의 말을 잊지 말며 어기지 말라 6 지혜를 버리지 말라 그가 너를 보호하리라 그를 사랑하라 그가 너를 지키리라 7 지혜가 제일이니 지혜를 얻으라 네가 얻은 모든 것을 가지고 명철을 얻을지니라 8 그를 높이라 그리하면 그가 너를 높이 들리라 만일 그를 품으면 그가 너를 영화롭게 하리라 9 그가 아름다운 관을 네 머리에 두겠고 영화로운 면류관을 네게 주리라 하셨느니라 10 내 아들아 들으라 내 말을 받으라 그리하면 네 생명의 해가 길리라

11 I instruct you in the way of wisdom and lead you along straight paths.

12 When you walk, your steps will not be hampered; when you run, you will not stumble.

13 Hold on to instruction, do not let it go; guard it well, for it is your life.

14 Do not set foot on the path of the wicked or walk in the way of evildoers.

15 Avoid it, do not travel on it; turn from it and go on your way.

16 For they cannot rest until they do evil; they are robbed of sleep till they make someone stumble.

17 They eat the bread of wickedness and drink the wine of violence.

18 The path of the righteous is like the morning sun, shining ever brighter till the full light of day.

19 But the way of the wicked is like deep darkness; they do not know what makes them stumble.

20 My son, pay attention to what I say; turn your ear to my words.

21 Do not let them out of your sight, keep them within your heart;

22 for they are life to those who find them and health to one's whole body.

11 내가 지혜로운 길을 네게 가르쳤으며 정직한 길로 너를 인도하였은즉 12 다닐 때에 네 걸음이 곤고하지 아니하겠고 달려갈 때에 실족하지 아니하리라 13 훈계를 굳게 잡아 놓치지 말고 지키라 이것이 네 생명이니라 14 사악한 자의 길에 들어가지 말며 악인의 길로 다니지 말지어다 15 그의 길을 피하고 지나가지 말며 돌이켜 떠나갈지어다 16 그들은 악을 행하지 못하면 자지 못하며 사람을 넘어뜨리지 못하면 잠이 오지 아니하며 17 불의의 떡을 먹으며 강포의 술을 마심이니라 18 의인의 길은 돋는 햇살 같아서 크게 빛나 한낮의 광명에 이르거니와 19 악인의 길은 어둠 같아서 그가 걸려 넘어져도 그것이 무엇인지 깨닫지 못하느니라 20 내 아들아 내 말에 주의하며 내가 말하는 것에 네 귀를 기울이라 21 그것을 네 눈에서 떠나게 하지 말며 네 마음 속에 지키라 22 그것은 얻는 자에게 생명이 되며 그의 온 육체의 건강이 됨이니라

23 Above all else, guard your heart, for everything you do flows from it.

24 Keep your mouth free of perversity; keep corrupt talk far from your lips.

25 Let your eyes look straight ahead; fix your gaze directly before you.

26 Give careful thought to the paths for your feet and be steadfast in all your ways.

27 Do not turn to the right or the left; keep your foot from evil.

Warning Against Adultery

1 My son, pay attention to my wisdom, turn your ear to my words of insight,

2 that you may maintain discretion and your lips may preserve knowledge.

3 For the lips of the adulterous woman drip honey, and her speech is smoother than oil;

4 but in the end she is bitter as gall, sharp as a double-edged sword.

5 Her feet go down to death; her steps lead straight to the grave.

6 She gives no thought to the way of life; her paths wander aimlessly, but she does not know it.

7 Now then, my sons, listen to me; do not turn aside from what I say.

8 Keep to a path far from her, do not go near the door of her house,

9 lest you lose your honor to others and your dignity to one who is cruel,

10 lest strangers feast on your wealth and your toil enrich the house of another.

11 At the end of your life you will groan, when your flesh and body are spent.

1 내 아들아 내 지혜에 주의하며 내 명철에 네 귀를 기울여서 2 근신을 지키며 네 입술로 지식을 지키도록 하라 3 대저 음녀의 입술은 꿀을 떨어뜨리며 그의 입은 기름보다 미끄러우나 4 나중은 쑥 같이 쓰고 두 날 가진 칼 같이 날카로우며 5 그의 발은 사지로 내려가며 그의 걸음은 스올로 나아가나니 6 그는 생명의 평탄한 길을 찾지 못하며 자기 길이 든든하지 못하여도 그것을 깨닫지 못하느니라 7 그런즉 아들들아 나에게 들으며 내 입의 말을 버리지 말고 8 네 길을 그에게서 멀리 하라 그의 집 문에도 가까이 가지 말라 9 두렵건대 네 존영이 남에게 잃어버리게 되며 네 수한이 잔인한 자에게 빼앗기게 될까 하노라 10 두렵건대 타인이 네 재물로 충족하게 되며 네 수고한 것이 외인의 집에 있게 될까 하노라 11 두렵건대 마지막에 이르러 네 몸, 네 육체가 쇠약할 때에 네가 한탄하여

12 You will say, "How I hated discipline! How my heart spurned correction!

13 I would not obey my teachers or turn my ear to my instructors.

14 And I was soon in serious trouble in the assembly of God's people."

15 Drink water from your own cistern, running water from your own well.

16 Should your springs overflow in the streets, your streams of water in the public squares?

17 Let them be yours alone, never to be shared with strangers.

18 May your fountain be blessed, and may you rejoice in the wife of your youth.

19 A loving doe, a graceful deer— may her breasts satisfy you always, may you ever be intoxicated with her love.

20 Why, my son, be intoxicated with another man's wife? Why embrace the bosom of a wayward woman?

21 For your ways are in full view of the Lord, and he examines all your paths.

22 The evil deeds of the wicked ensnare them; the cords of their sins hold them fast.

23 For lack of discipline they will die, led astray by their own great folly.

12 말하기를 내가 어찌하여 훈계를 싫어하며 내 마음이 꾸지람을 가벼이 여기고 13 내 선생의 목소리를 청종하지 아니하며 나를 가르치는 이에게 귀를 기울이지 아니하였던고 14 많은 무리들이 모인 중에서 큰 악에 빠지게 되었노라 하게 될까 염려하노라 15 너는 네 우물에서 물을 마시며 네 샘에서 흐르는 물을 마시라 16 어찌하여 네 샘물을 집 밖으로 넘치게 하며 네 도랑물을 거리로 흘러가게 하겠느냐 17 그 물이 네게만 있게 하고 타인과 더불어 그것을 나누지 말라 18 네 샘으로 복되게 하라 네가 젊어서 취한 아내를 즐거워하라 19 그는 사랑스러운 암사슴 같고 아름다운 암노루 같으니 너는 그의 품을 항상 족하게 여기며 그의 사랑을 항상 연모하라 20 내 아들아 어찌하여 음녀를 연모하겠으며 어찌하여 이방 계집의 가슴을 안겠느냐 21 대저 사람의 길은 여호와의 눈 앞에 있나니 그가 그 사람의 모든 길을 평탄하게 하시느니라 22 악인은 자기의 악에 걸리며 그 죄의 줄에 매이나니 23 그는 훈계를 받지 아니함으로 말미암아 죽겠고 심히 미련함으로 말미암아 혼미하게 되느니라

미리보는 어휘

9장

abuse 모욕
correct 징계하다, 꾸짖다
folly 어리석음
undisciplined 규율없는
incur 초래하다
judgment 판결, 심판
mocker 조롱하는 자
rebuke 꾸짖다
hew out 쪼아서 만들다
pass by : 지나가다

10장

chattering 잡담하는
craving 욕망
crooked 구부러진
discerning 통찰력있는
ill-gotten 부정한 수단을 얻은
integrity 성실
maliciously 부당하게
overwhelm 압도하다
thwart 좌절시키다
conceal 숨기다
discipline 훈계
dread 두려워하다
nourish 영양을 공급하다
perverse 사악한
uproot 뿌리를 뽑다
come to ruin : 파멸에 이르다
stir up : 부추기다, 일으키다
lead A astray : A를 나쁜 길로 이끌다

Warning Against Folly

1 My son, if you have put up security for your neighbor, if you have struck hands in pledge for a another,

2 you have been trapped by what you said, ensnared by the words of your mouth.

3 So do this, my son, to free yourself, since you have fallen into your neighbor's hands: Go—to the point of exhaustion— and give your neighbor no rest!

4 Allow no sleep to your eyes, no slumber to your eyelids.

5 Free yourself, like a gazelle from the hand of the hunter, like a bird from the snare of the fowler.

6 Go to the ant, you sluggard; consider its ways and be wise!

7 It has no commander, no overseer or ruler,

8 yet it stores its provisions in summer and gathers its food at harvest.

9 How long will you lie there, you sluggard? When will you get up from your sleep?

10 A little sleep, a little slumber, a little folding of the hands to rest—

11 and poverty will come on you like a thief and scarcity like an armed man.

1 내 아들아 네가 만일 이웃을 위하여 담보하며 타인을 위하여 보증하였으면 2 네 입의 말로 네가 얽혔으며 네 입의 말로 인하여 잡히게 되었느니라 3 내 아들아 네가 네 이웃의 손에 빠졌은즉 이같이 하라 너는 곧 가서 겸손히 네 이웃에게 간구하여 스스로 구원하되 4 네 눈을 잠들게 하지 말며 눈꺼풀을 감기게 하지 말고 5 노루가 사냥꾼의 손에서 벗어나는 것 같이, 새가 그물 치는 자의 손에서 벗어나는 것 같이 스스로 구원하라 6 게으른 자여 개미에게 가서 그가 하는 것을 보고 지혜를 얻으라 7 개미는 두령도 없고 감독자도 없고 통치자도 없으되 8 먹을 것을 여름 동안에 예비하며 추수 때에 양식을 모으느니라 9 게으른 자여 네가 어느 때까지 누워 있겠느냐 네가 어느 때에 잠이 깨어 일어나겠느냐 10 좀더 자자, 좀더 졸자, 손을 모으고 좀더 누워 있자 하면 11 네 빈궁이 강도 같이 오며 네 곤핍이 군사 같이 이르리라

12 A troublemaker and a villain, who goes about with a corrupt mouth,

13 who winks maliciously with his eye, signals with his feet and motions with his fingers,

14 who plots evil with deceit in his heart—he always stirs up conflict.

15 Therefore disaster will overtake him in an instant; he will suddenly be destroyed—without remedy.

16 There are six things the Lord hates, seven that are detestable to him:

17 haughty eyes, a lying tongue, hands that shed innocent blood,

18 a heart that devises wicked schemes, feet that are quick to rush into evil,

19 a false witness who pours out lies and a person who stirs up conflict in the community.

Warning Against Adultery

20 My son, keep your father's command and do not forsake your mother's teaching.

21 Bind them always on your heart; fasten them around your neck.

22 When you walk, they will guide you; when you sleep, they will watch over you; when you awake, they will speak to you.

23 For this command is a lamp, this teaching is a light, and correction and instruction are the way to life,

12 불량하고 악한 자는 구부러진 말을 하고 다니며 13 눈짓을 하며 발로 뜻을 보이며 손가락질을 하며 14 그의 마음에 패역을 품으며 항상 악을 꾀하여 다툼을 일으키는 자라 15 그러므로 그의 재앙이 갑자기 내려 당장에 멸망하여 살릴 길이 없으리라 16 여호와께서 미워하시는 것 곧 그의 마음에 싫어하시는 것이 예닐곱 가지이니 17 곧 교만한 눈과 거짓된 혀와 무죄한 자의 피를 흘리는 손과 18 악한 계교를 꾀하는 마음과 빨리 악으로 달려가는 발과 19 거짓을 말하는 망령된 증인과 및 형제 사이를 이간하는 자이니라 20 내 아들아 네 아비의 명령을 지키며 네 어미의 법을 떠나지 말고 21 그것을 항상 네 마음에 새기며 네 목에 매라 22 그것이 네가 다닐 때에 너를 인도하며 네가 잘 때에 너를 보호하며 네가 깰 때에 너와 더불어 말하리니 23 대저 명령은 등불이요 법은 빛이요 훈계의 책망은 곧 생명의 길이라

24 keeping you from your neighbor's wife, from the smooth talk of a wayward woman.

25 Do not lust in your heart after her beauty or let her captivate you with her eyes.

26 For a prostitute can be had for a loaf of bread, but another man's wife preys on your very life.

27 Can a man scoop fire into his lap without his clothes being burned?

28 Can a man walk on hot coals without his feet being scorched?

29 So is he who sleeps with another man's wife; no one who touches her will go unpunished.

30 People do not despise a thief if he steals to satisfy his hunger when he is starving.

31 Yet if he is caught, he must pay sevenfold, though it costs him all the wealth of his house.

32 But a man who commits adultery has no sense; whoever does so destroys himself.

33 Blows and disgrace are his lot, and his shame will never be wiped away.

34 For jealousy arouses a husband's fury, and he will show no mercy when he takes revenge.

35 He will not accept any compensation; he will refuse a bribe, however great it is.

24 이것이 너를 지켜 악한 여인에게, 이방 여인의 혀로 호리는 말에 빠지지 않게 하리라 25 네 마음에 그의 아름다움을 탐하지 말며 그 눈꺼풀에 홀리지 말라 26 음녀로 말미암아 사람이 한 조각 떡만 남게 됨이며 음란한 여인은 귀한 생명을 사냥함이니라 27 사람이 불을 품에 품고서야 어찌 그의 옷이 타지 아니하겠으며 28 사람이 숯불을 밟고서야 어찌 그의 발이 데지 아니하겠느냐 29 남의 아내와 통간하는 자도 이와 같을 것이라 그를 만지는 자마다 벌을 면하지 못하리라 30 도둑이 만일 주릴 때에 배를 채우려고 도둑질하면 사람이 그를 멸시하지는 아니하려니와 31 들키면 칠 배를 갚아야 하리니 심지어 자기 집에 있는 것을 다 내주게 되리라 32 여인과 간음하는 자는 무지한 자라 이것을 행하는 자는 자기의 영혼을 망하게 하며 33 상함과 능욕을 받고 부끄러움을 씻을 수 없게 되나니 34 남편이 투기로 분노하여 원수 갚는 날에 용서하지 아니하고 35 어떤 보상도 받지 아니하며 많은 선물을 줄지라도 듣지 아니하리라

Warning Against the Adulterous Woman

1 My son, keep my words and store up my commands within you.

2 Keep my commands and you will live; guard my teachings as the apple of your eye.

3 Bind them on your fingers; write them on the tablet of your heart.

4 Say to wisdom, "You are my sister," and to insight, "You are my relative."

5 They will keep you from the adulterous woman, from the wayward woman with her seductive words.

6 At the window of my house I looked down through the lattice.

7 I saw among the simple, I noticed among the young men, a youth who had no sense.

8 He was going down the street near her corner, walking along in the direction of her house

9 at twilight, as the day was fading, as the dark of night set in.

10 Then out came a woman to meet him, dressed like a prostitute and with crafty intent.

11 (She is unruly and defiant, her feet never stay at home;

12 now in the street, now in the squares, at every corner she lurks.)

1 내 아들아 내 말을 지키며 내 계명을 간직하라 2 내 계명을 지켜 살며 내 법을 네 눈동자처럼 지키라 3 이것을 네 손가락에 매며 이것을 네 마음판에 새기라 4 지혜에게 너는 내 누이라 하며 명철에게 너는 내 친족이라 하라 5 그리하면 이것이 너를 지켜서 음녀에게, 말로 호리는 이방 여인에게 빠지지 않게 하리라 6 내가 내 집 들창으로, 살창으로 내다 보다가 7 어리석은 자 중에, 젊은이 가운데에 한 지혜 없는 자를 보았노라 8 그가 거리를 지나 음녀의 골목 모퉁이로 가까이 하여 그의 집쪽으로 가는데 9 저물 때, 황혼 때, 깊은 밤 흑암 중에라 10 그 때에 기생의 옷을 입은 간교한 여인이 그를 맞으니 11 이 여인은 떠들며 완악하며 그의 발이 집에 머물지 아니하여 12 어떤 때에는 거리, 어떤 때에는 광장 또 모퉁이마다 서서 사람을 기다리는 자라

13 She took hold of him and kissed him and with a brazen face
she said:

14 "Today I fulfilled my vows, and I have food from my fellowship
offering at home.

15 So I came out to meet you; I looked for you and have found
you!

16 I have covered my bed with colored linens from Egypt.

17 I have perfumed my bed with myrrh, aloes and cinnamon.

18 Come, let's drink deeply of love till morning; let's enjoy
ourselves with love!

19 My husband is not at home; he has gone on a long journey.

20 He took his purse filled with money and will not be home till
full moon."

21 With persuasive words she led him astray; she seduced him
with her smooth talk.

22 All at once he followed her like an ox going to the slaughter,
like a deer stepping into a noose

23 till an arrow pierces his liver, like a bird darting into a snare,
little knowing it will cost him his life.

24 Now then, my sons, listen to me; pay attention to what I say.

25 Do not let your heart turn to her ways or stray into her paths.

26 Many are the victims she has brought down; her slain are a
mighty throng.

27 Her house is a highway to the grave, leading down to the
chambers of death.

---

13 그 여인이 그를 붙잡고 그에게 입맞추며 부끄러움을 모르는 얼굴로 그에게 말하되 14 내가 화목제를 드려 서원한 것을 오늘 갚
았노라 15 이러므로 내가 너를 맞으려고 나와 네 얼굴을 찾다가 너를 만났도다 16 내 침상에는 요와 애굽의 무늬 있는 이불을 폈
고 17 몰약과 침향과 계피를 뿌렸노라 18 오라 우리가 아침까지 흡족하게 서로 사랑하며 사랑함으로 희락하자 19 남편은 집을 떠
나 먼 길을 갔는데 20 은 주머니를 가졌은즉 보름 날에나 집에 돌아오리라 하여 21 여러 가지 고운 말로 유혹하며 입술의 호리는
말로 꾀므로 22 젊은이가 곧 그를 따랐으니 소가 도수장으로 가는 것 같고 미련한 자가 벌을 받으려고 쇠사슬에 매이러 가는 것과
같도다 23 필경은 화살이 그 간을 뚫게 되리라 새가 빨리 그물로 들어가되 그의 생명을 잃어버릴 줄을 알지 못함과 같으니라 24 이
제 아들들아 내 말을 듣고 내 입의 말에 주의하라 25 네 마음이 음녀의 길로 치우치지 말며 그 길에 미혹되지 말지어다 26 대저 그
가 많은 사람을 상하여 엎드러지게 하였나니 그에게 죽은 자가 허다하니라 27 그의 집은 스올의 길이라 사망의 방으로 내려가느니라

proverbs
8

Wisdom's Call

1 Does not wisdom call out? Does not understanding raise her voice?

2 At the highest point along the way, where the paths meet, she takes her stand;

3 beside the gate leading into the city, at the entrance, she cries aloud:

4 "To you, O people, I call out; I raise my voice to all mankind.

5 You who are simple, gain prudence; you who are foolish, set your hearts on it.

6 Listen, for I have trustworthy things to say; I open my lips to speak what is right.

7 My mouth speaks what is true, for my lips detest wickedness.

8 All the words of my mouth are just; none of them is crooked or perverse.

9 To the discerning all of them are right; they are upright to those who have found knowledge.

10 Choose my instruction instead of silver, knowledge rather than choice gold,

1 지혜가 부르지 아니하느냐 명철이 소리를 높이지 아니하느냐 2 그가 길 가의 높은 곳과 네거리에 서며 3 성문 곁과 문 어귀와 여러 출입하는 문에서 불러 이르되 4 사람들아 내가 너희를 부르며 내가 인자들에게 소리를 높이노라 5 어리석은 자들아 너희는 명철할지니라 미련한 자들아 너희는 마음이 밝을지니라 6 너희는 들을지어다 내가 가장 선한 것을 말하리라 내 입술을 열어 정직을 내리라 7 내 입은 진리를 말하며 내 입술은 악을 미워하느니라 8 내 입의 말은 다 의로운즉 그 가운데에 굽은 것과 패역한 것이 없나니 9 이는 다 총명 있는 자가 밝히 아는 바요 지식 얻은 자가 정직하게 여기는 바니라 10 너희가 은을 받지 말고 나의 훈계를 받으며 정금보다 지식을 얻으라

11 for wisdom is more precious than rubies, and nothing you desire can compare with her.

12 "I, wisdom, dwell together with prudence; I possess knowledge and discretion.

13 To fear the Lord is to hate evil; I hate pride and arrogance, evil behavior and perverse speech.

14 Counsel and sound judgment are mine; I have insight, I have power.

15 By me kings reign and rulers issue decrees that are just;

16 by me princes govern, and nobles—all who rule on earth.

17 I love those who love me, and those who seek me find me.

18 With me are riches and honor, enduring wealth and prosperity.

19 My fruit is better than fine gold; what I yield surpasses choice silver.

20 I walk in the way of righteousness, along the paths of justice,

21 bestowing a rich inheritance on those who love me and making their treasuries full.

22 "The Lord brought me forth as the first of his works, before his deeds of old;

23 I was formed long ages ago, at the very beginning, when the world came to be.

24 When there were no watery depths, I was given birth, when there were no springs overflowing with water;

11 대저 지혜는 진주보다 나으므로 원하는 모든 것을 이에 비교할 수 없음이니라 12 나 지혜는 명철로 주소를 삼으며 지식과 근신을 찾아 얻나니 13 여호와를 경외하는 것은 악을 미워하는 것이라 나는 교만과 거만과 악한 행실과 패역한 입을 미워하느니라 14 내게는 계략과 참 지식이 있으며 나는 명철이라 내게 능력이 있으므로 15 나로 말미암아 왕들이 치리하며 방백들이 공의를 세우며 16 나로 말미암아 재상과 존귀한 자 곧 모든 의로운 재판관들이 다스리느니라 17 나를 사랑하는 자들이 나의 사랑을 입으며 나를 간절히 찾는 자가 나를 만날 것이니라 18 부귀가 내게 있고 장구한 재물과 공의도 그러하니라 19 내 열매는 금이나 정금보다 나으며 내 소득은 순은보다 나으니라 20 나는 정의로운 길로 행하며 공의로운 길 가운데로 다니나니 21 이는 나를 사랑하는 자가 재물을 얻어서 그 곳간에 채우게 하려 함이니라 22 여호와께서 그 조화의 시작 곧 태초에 일하시기 전에 나를 가지셨으며 23 만세 전부터, 태초부터, 땅이 생기기 전부터 내가 세움을 받았나니 24 아직 바다가 생기지 아니하였고 큰 샘들이 있기 전에 내가 이미 났으며

25 before the mountains were settled in place, before the hills,
I was given birth,

26 before he made the world or its fields or any of the dust of the
earth.

27 I was there when he set the heavens in place, when he marked
out the horizon on the face of the deep,

28 when he established the clouds above and fixed securely the
fountains of the deep,

29 when he gave the sea its boundary so the waters would
not overstep his command, and when he marked out the
foundations of the earth.

30 Then I was constantly at his side. I was filled with delight day
after day, rejoicing always in his presence,

31 rejoicing in his whole world and delighting in mankind.

32 "Now then, my children, listen to me; blessed are those who
keep my ways.

33 Listen to my instruction and be wise; do not disregard it.

34 Blessed are those who listen to me, watching daily at my doors,
waiting at my doorway.

35 For those who find me find life and receive favor from the
Lord.

36 But those who fail to find me harm themselves; all who hate
me love death."

25 산이 세워지기 전에, 언덕이 생기기 전에 내가 이미 났으니 26 하나님이 아직 땅도, 들도, 세상 진토의 근원도 짓지 아니하셨을 때에라 27 그가 하늘을 지으시며 궁창을 해면에 두르실 때에 내가 거기 있었고 28 그가 위로 구름 하늘을 견고하게 하시며 바다의 샘들을 힘 있게 하시며 29 바다의 한계를 정하여 물이 명령을 거스르지 못하게 하시며 또 땅의 기초를 정하실 때에 30 내가 그 곁에 있어서 창조자가 되어 날마다 그의 기뻐하신 바가 되었으며 항상 그 앞에서 즐거워하였으며 31 사람이 거처할 땅에서 즐거워하며 인자들을 기뻐하였느니라 32 아들들아 이제 내게 들으라 내 도를 지키는 자가 복이 있느니라 33 훈계를 들어서 지혜를 얻으라 그것을 버리지 말라 34 누구든지 내게 들으며 날마다 내 문 곁에서 기다리며 문설주 옆에서 기다리는 자는 복이 있나니 35 대저 나를 얻는 자는 생명을 얻고 여호와께 은총을 얻을 것임이니라 36 그러나 나를 잃는 자는 자기의 영혼을 해하는 자라 나를 미워하는 자는 사망을 사랑하느니라

Invitations of Wisdom and Folly

1 Wisdom has built her house; she has set up its seven pillars.

2 She has prepared her meat and mixed her wine; she has also set her table.

3 She has sent out her servants, and she calls from the highest point of the city,

4 "Let all who are simple come to my house!" To those who have no sense she says,

5 "Come, eat my food and drink the wine I have mixed.

6 Leave your simple ways and you will live; walk in the way of insight."

7 Whoever corrects a mocker invites insults; whoever rebukes the wicked incurs abuse.

8 Do not rebuke mockers or they will hate you; rebuke the wise and they will love you.

9 Instruct the wise and they will be wiser still; teach the righteous and they will add to their learning.

10 The fear of the Lord is the beginning of wisdom, and knowledge of the Holy One is understanding.

11 For through wisdom your days will be many, and years will be added to your life.

12 If you are wise, your wisdom will reward you; if you are a mocker, you alone will suffer.

13 Folly is an unruly woman; she is simple and knows nothing.

14 She sits at the door of her house, on a seat at the highest point of the city,

15 calling out to those who pass by, who go straight on their way,

16 "Let all who are simple come to my house!" To those who have no sense she says,

17 "Stolen water is sweet; food eaten in secret is delicious!"

18 But little do they know that the dead are there, that her guests are deep in the realm of the dead.

11 나 지혜로 말미암아 네 날이 많아질 것이요 네 생명의 해가 네게 더하리라 12 네가 만일 지혜로우면 그 지혜가 네게 유익할 것이나 네가 만일 거만하면 너 홀로 해를 당하리라 13 미련한 여인이 떠들며 어리석어서 아무것도 알지 못하고 14 자기 집 문에 앉으며 성읍 높은 곳에 있는 자리에 앉아서 15 자기 길을 바로 가는 행인들을 불러 이르되 16 어리석은 자는 이리로 돌이키라 또 지혜 없는 자에게 이르기를 17 도둑질한 물이 달고 몰래 먹는 떡이 맛이 있다 하는도다 18 오직 그 어리석은 자는 죽은 자들이 거기 있는 것과 그의 객들이 스올 깊은 곳에 있는 것을 알지 못하느니라

Proverbs of Solomon

1 The proverbs of Solomon: A wise son brings joy to his father, but a foolish son brings grief to his mother.

2 Ill-gotten treasures have no lasting value, but righteousness delivers from death.

3 The Lord does not let the righteous go hungry, but he thwarts the craving of the wicked.

4 Lazy hands make for poverty, but diligent hands bring wealth.

5 He who gathers crops in summer is a prudent son, but he who sleeps during harvest is a disgraceful son.

6 Blessings crown the head of the righteous, but violence overwhelms the mouth of the wicked.

7 The name of the righteous is used in blessings, but the name of the wicked will rot.

8 The wise in heart accept commands, but a chattering fool comes to ruin.

9 Whoever walks in integrity walks securely, but whoever takes crooked paths will be found out.

10 Whoever winks maliciously causes grief, and a chattering fool comes to ruin.

1 솔로몬의 잠언이라 지혜로운 아들은 아비를 기쁘게 하거니와 미련한 아들은 어미의 근심이니라 2 불의의 재물은 무익하여도 공의는 죽음에서 건지느니라 3 여호와께서 의인의 영혼은 주리지 않게 하시나 악인의 소욕은 물리치시느니라 4 손을 게으르게 놀리는 자는 가난하게 되고 손이 부지런한 자는 부하게 되느니라 5 여름에 거두는 자는 지혜로운 아들이나 추수 때에 자는 자는 부끄러움을 끼치는 아들이니라 6 의인의 머리에는 복이 임하나 악인의 입은 독을 머금었느니라 7 의인을 기념할 때에는 칭찬하거니와 악인의 이름은 썩게 되느니라 8 마음이 지혜로운 자는 계명을 받거니와 입이 미련한 자는 멸망하리라 9 바른 길로 행하는 자는 걸음이 평안하려니와 굽은 길로 행하는 자는 드러나리라 10 눈짓하는 자는 근심을 끼치고 입이 미련한 자는 멸망하느니라

11 The mouth of the righteous is a fountain of life, but the mouth of the wicked conceals violence.

12 Hatred stirs up conflict, but love covers over all wrongs.

13 Wisdom is found on the lips of the discerning, but a rod is for the back of one who has no sense.

14 The wise store up knowledge, but the mouth of a fool invites ruin.

15 The wealth of the rich is their fortified city, but poverty is the ruin of the poor.

16 The wages of the righteous is life, but the earnings of the wicked are sin and death.

17 Whoever heeds discipline shows the way to life, but whoever ignores correction leads others astray.

18 Whoever conceals hatred with lying lips and spreads slander is a fool.

19 Sin is not ended by multiplying words, but the prudent hold their tongues.

20 The tongue of the righteous is choice silver, but the heart of the wicked is of little value.

21 The lips of the righteous nourish many, but fools die for lack of sense.

22 The blessing of the Lord brings wealth, without painful toil for it.

23 A fool finds pleasure in wicked schemes, but a person of understanding delights in wisdom.

24 What the wicked dread will overtake them; what the righteous desire will be granted.

25 When the storm has swept by, the wicked are gone, but the righteous stand firm forever.

26 As vinegar to the teeth and smoke to the eyes, so are sluggards to those who send them.

27 The fear of the Lord adds length to life, but the years of the wicked are cut short.

28 The prospect of the righteous is joy, but the hopes of the wicked come to nothing.

29 The way of the Lord is a refuge for the blameless, but it is the ruin of those who do evil.

30 The righteous will never be uprooted, but the wicked will not remain in the land.

31 From the mouth of the righteous comes the fruit of wisdom, but a perverse tongue will be silenced.

32 The lips of the righteous know what finds favor, but the mouth of the wicked only what is perverse.

14장

bitterness 비통
crafty 간교한
deceitful 속이는
flourish 번성하다
fortress 요새
hotheaded 성급한
quick-tempered 성미급한
shun 피하다
incur 유발하다
repose …에 있다
devious 악한
discerning 총명한
exalt 높이다
rot 썩게 하다
tear down : 부수다, 해체하다
pour out : 쏟아내다
mock at... : …를 조롱하다, 놀리다
go astray : 길을 잃다, 타락하다

15장

discerning 총명한
gush 쏟아내다
harsh 가혹한
prudence 사려 분별
turmoil 불안
wretched 비참한
bribe 뇌물
discipline 훈계
dissension 불화
fatten 살찌우다
greedy 탐욕스러운
hot-tempered 화 잘내는
intact 손대지 않은
thorn 가시
stir up : 불러 일으키다
tear down : 헐다, 부수다

1 The LORD detests dishonest scales, but accurate weights find favor with him.

2 When pride comes, then comes disgrace, but with humility comes wisdom.

3 The integrity of the upright guides them, but the unfaithful are destroyed by their duplicity.

4 Wealth is worthless in the day of wrath, but righteousness delivers from death.

5 The righteousness of the blameless makes their paths straight, but the wicked are brought down by their own wickedness.

6 The righteousness of the upright delivers them, but the unfaithful are trapped by evil desires.

7 Hopes placed in mortals die with them; all the promise of their power comes to nothing.

8 The righteous person is rescued from trouble, and it falls on the wicked instead.

9 With their mouths the godless destroy their neighbors, but through knowledge the righteous escape.

10 When the righteous prosper, the city rejoices; when the wicked perish, there are shouts of joy.

1 속이는 저울은 여호와께서 미워하시나 공평한 추는 그가 기뻐하시느니라 2 교만이 오면 욕도 오거니와 겸손한 자에게는 지혜가 있느니라 3 정직한 자의 성실은 자기를 인도하거니와 사악한 자의 패역은 자기를 망하게 하느니라 4 재물은 진노하시는 날에 무익하나 공의는 죽음에서 건지느니라 5 완전한 자의 공의는 자기의 길을 곧게 하려니와 악한 자는 자기의 악으로 말미암아 넘어지리라 6 정직한 자의 공의는 자기를 건지려니와 사악한 자는 자기의 악에 잡히리라 7 악인은 죽을 때에 그 소망이 끊어지나니 불의의 소망이 없어지느니라 8 의인은 환난에서 구원을 얻으나 악인은 자기의 길로 가느니라 9 악인은 입으로 그의 이웃을 망하게 하여도 의인은 그의 지식으로 말미암아 구원을 얻느니라 10 의인이 형통하면 성읍이 즐거워하고 악인이 패망하면 기뻐 외치느니라

11 Through the blessing of the upright a city is exalted, but by the mouth of the wicked it is destroyed.

12 Whoever derides their neighbor has no sense, but the one who has understanding holds their tongue.

13 A gossip betrays a confidence, but a trustworthy person keeps a secret.

14 For lack of guidance a nation falls, but victory is won through many advisers.

15 Whoever puts up security for a stranger will surely suffer, but whoever refuses to shake hands in pledge is safe.

16 A kindhearted woman gains honor, but ruthless men gain only wealth.

17 Those who are kind benefit themselves, but the cruel bring ruin on themselves.

18 A wicked person earns deceptive wages, but the one who sows righteousness reaps a sure reward.

19 Truly the righteous attain life, but whoever pursues evil finds death.

20 The Lord detests those whose hearts are perverse, but he delights in those whose ways are blameless.

21 Be sure of this: The wicked will not go unpunished, but those who are righteous will go free.

11 성읍은 정직한 자의 축복으로 인하여 진흥하고 악한 자의 입으로 말미암아 무너지느니라 12 지혜 없는 자는 그의 이웃을 멸시하나 명철한 자는 잠잠하느니라 13 두루 다니며 한담하는 자는 남의 비밀을 누설하나 마음이 신실한 자는 그런 것을 숨기느니라 14 지략이 없으면 백성이 망하여도 지략이 많으면 평안을 누리느니라 15 타인을 위하여 보증이 되는 자는 손해를 당하여도 보증되기를 싫어하는 자는 평안하느니라 16 유덕한 여자는 존영을 얻고 근면한 남자는 재물을 얻느니라 17 인자한 자는 자기의 영혼을 이롭게 하고 잔인한 자는 자기의 몸을 해롭게 하느니라 18 악인의 삯은 허무하되 공의를 뿌린 자의 상은 확실하니라 19 공의를 굳게 지키는 자는 생명에 이르고 악을 따르는 자는 사망에 이르느니라 20 마음이 굽은 자는 여호와께 미움을 받아도 행위가 온전한 자는 그의 기뻐하심을 받느니라 21 악인은 피차 손을 잡을지라도 벌을 면하지 못할 것이나 의인의 자손은 구원을 얻으리라

22 Like a gold ring in a pig's snout is a beautiful woman who shows no discretion.

23 The desire of the righteous ends only in good, but the hope of the wicked only in wrath.

24 One person gives freely, yet gains even more; another withholds unduly, but comes to poverty.

25 A generous person will prosper; whoever refreshes others will be refreshed.

26 People curse the one who hoards grain, but they pray God's blessing on the one who is willing to sell.

27 Whoever seeks good finds favor, but evil comes to one who searches for it.

28 Those who trust in their riches will fall, but the righteous will thrive like a green leaf.

29 Whoever brings ruin on their family will inherit only wind, and the fool will be servant to the wise.

30 The fruit of the righteous is a tree of life, and the one who is wise saves lives.

31 If the righteous receive their due on earth, how much more the ungodly and the sinner!

1   Whoever loves discipline loves knowledge, but whoever hates correction is stupid.

2   Good people obtain favor from the Lord, but he condemns those who devise wicked schemes.

3   No one can be established through wickedness, but the righteous cannot be uprooted.

4   A wife of noble character is her husband's crown, but a disgraceful wife is like decay in his bones.

5   The plans of the righteous are just, but the advice of the wicked is deceitful.

6   The words of the wicked lie in wait for blood, but the speech of the upright rescues them.

7   The wicked are overthrown and are no more, but the house of the righteous stands firm.

8   A person is praised according to their prudence, and one with a warped mind is despised.

9   Better to be a nobody and yet have a servant than pretend to be somebody and have no food.

10 The righteous care for the needs of their animals, but the kindest acts of the wicked are cruel.

1 훈계를 좋아하는 자는 지식을 좋아하거니와 징계를 싫어하는 자는 짐승과 같으니라 2 선인은 여호와께 은총을 받으려니와 악을 꾀하는 자는 정죄하심을 받으리라 3 사람이 악으로서 굳게 서지 못하거니와 의인의 뿌리는 움직이지 아니하느니라 4 어진 여인은 그 지아비의 면류관이나 욕을 끼치는 여인은 그 지아비의 뼈가 썩음 같게 하느니라 5 의인의 생각은 정직하여도 악인의 도모는 속임이니라 6 악인의 말은 사람을 엿보아 피를 흘리자 하는 것이거니와 정직한 자의 입은 사람을 구원하느니라 7 악인은 엎드러져서 소멸되려니와 의인의 집은 서 있으리라 8 사람은 그 지혜대로 칭찬을 받으려니와 마음이 굽은 자는 멸시를 받으리라 9 비천히 여김을 받을지라도 종을 부리는 자는 스스로 높은 체하고도 음식이 핍절한 자보다 나으니라 10 의인은 자기의 가축의 생명을 돌보나 악인의 긍휼은 잔인이니라

11 Those who work their land will have abundant food, but those who chase fantasies have no sense.

12 The wicked desire the stronghold of evildoers, but the root of the righteous endures.

13 Evildoers are trapped by their sinful talk, and so the innocent escape trouble.

14 From the fruit of their lips people are filled with good things, and the work of their hands brings them reward.

15 The way of fools seems right to them, but the wise listen to advice.

16 Fools show their annoyance at once, but the prudent overlook an insult.

17 An honest witness tells the truth, but a false witness tells lies.

18 The words of the reckless pierce like swords, but the tongue of the wise brings healing.

19 Truthful lips endure forever, but a lying tongue lasts only a moment.

20 Deceit is in the hearts of those who plot evil, but those who promote peace have joy.

21 No harm overtakes the righteous, but the wicked have their fill of trouble.

11 자기의 토지를 경작하는 자는 먹을 것이 많거니와 방탕한 것을 따르는 자는 지혜가 없느니라 12 악인은 불의의 이익을 탐하나 의인은 그 뿌리로 말미암아 결실하느니라 13 악인은 입술의 허물로 말미암아 그물에 걸려도 의인은 환난에서 벗어나느니라 14 사람은 입의 열매로 말미암아 복록에 족하며 그 손이 행하는 대로 자기가 받느니라 15 미련한 자는 자기 행위를 바른 줄로 여기나 지혜로운 자는 권고를 듣느니라 16 미련한 자는 당장 분노를 나타내거니와 슬기로운 자는 수욕을 참느니라 17 진리를 말하는 자는 의를 나타내어도 거짓 증인은 속이는 말을 하느니라 18 칼로 찌름 같이 함부로 말하는 자가 있거니와 지혜로운 자의 혀는 양약과 같으니라 19 진실한 입술은 영원히 보존되거니와 거짓 혀는 잠시 동안만 있을 뿐이니라 20 악을 꾀하는 자의 마음에는 속임이 있고 화평을 의논하는 자에게는 희락이 있느니라 21 의인에게는 어떤 재앙도 임하지 아니하려니와 악인에게는 앙화가 가득하리라

22 The LORD detests lying lips, but he delights in people who are trustworthy.

23 The prudent keep their knowledge to themselves, but a fool's heart blurts out folly.

24 Diligent hands will rule, but laziness ends in forced labor.

25 Anxiety weighs down the heart, but a kind word cheers it up.

26 The righteous choose their friends carefully, but the way of the wicked leads them astray.

27 The lazy do not roast any game, but the diligent feed on the riches of the hunt.

28 In the way of righteousness there is life; along that path is immortality.

22 거짓 입술은 여호와께 미움을 받아도 진실하게 행하는 자는 그의 기뻐하심을 받느니라 23 슬기로운 자는 지식을 감추어도 미련한 자의 마음은 미련한 것을 전파하느니라 24 부지런한 자의 손은 사람을 다스리게 되어도 게으른 자는 부림을 받느니라 25 근심이 사람의 마음에 있으면 그것으로 번뇌하게 되나 선한 말은 그것을 즐겁게 하느니라 26 의인은 그 이웃의 인도자가 되나 악인의 소행은 자신을 미혹하느니라 27 게으른 자는 그 잡을 것도 사냥하지 아니하나니 사람의 부귀는 부지런한 것이니라 28 공의로운 길에 생명이 있나니 그 길에는 사망이 없느니라

1 A wise son heeds his father's instruction, but a mocker does not respond to rebukes.

2 From the fruit of their lips people enjoy good things, but the unfaithful have an appetite for violence.

3 Those who guard their lips preserve their lives, but those who speak rashly will come to ruin.

4 A sluggard's appetite is never filled, but the desires of the diligent are fully satisfied.

5 The righteous hate what is false, but the wicked make themselves a stench and bring shame on themselves.

6 Righteousness guards the person of integrity, but wickedness overthrows the sinner.

7 One person pretends to be rich, yet has nothing; another pretends to be poor, yet has great wealth.

8 A person's riches may ransom their life, but the poor cannot respond to threatening rebukes.

9 The light of the righteous shines brightly, but the lamp of the wicked is snuffed out.

10 Where there is strife, there is pride, but wisdom is found in those who take advice.

1 지혜로운 아들은 아비의 훈계를 들으나 거만한 자는 꾸지람을 즐겨 듣지 아니하느니라 2 사람은 입의 열매로 인하여 복록을 누리거니와 마음이 궤사한 자는 강포를 당하느니라 3 입을 지키는 자는 자기의 생명을 보전하나 입술을 크게 벌리는 자에게는 멸망이 오느니라 4 게으른 자는 마음으로 원하여도 얻지 못하나 부지런한 자의 마음은 풍족함을 얻느니라 5 의인은 거짓말을 미워하나 악인은 행위가 흉악하여 부끄러운 데에 이르느니라 6 공의는 행실이 정직한 자를 보호하고 악은 죄인을 패망하게 하느니라 7 스스로 부한 체하여도 아무 것도 없는 자가 있고 스스로 가난한 체하여도 재물이 많은 자가 있느니라 8 사람의 재물이 자기 생명의 속전일 수 있으나 가난한 자는 협박을 받을 일이 없느니라 9 의인의 빛은 환하게 빛나고 악인의 등불은 꺼지느니라 10 교만에서는 다툼만 일어날 뿐이라 권면을 듣는 자는 지혜가 있느니라

11 Dishonest money dwindles away, but whoever gathers money little by little makes it grow.

12 Hope deferred makes the heart sick, but a longing fulfilled is a tree of life.

13 Whoever scorns instruction will pay for it, but whoever respects a command is rewarded.

14 The teaching of the wise is a fountain of life, turning a person from the snares of death.

15 Good judgment wins favor, but the way of the unfaithful leads to their destruction.

16 All who are prudent act with knowledge, but fools expose their folly.

17 A wicked messenger falls into trouble, but a trustworthy envoy brings healing.

18 Whoever disregards discipline comes to poverty and shame, but whoever heeds correction is honored.

19 A longing fulfilled is sweet to the soul, but fools detest turning from evil.

20 Walk with the wise and become wise, for a companion of fools suffers harm.

21 Trouble pursues the sinner, but the righteous are rewarded with good things.

11 망령되이 얻은 재물은 줄어가고 손으로 모은 것은 늘어가느니라 12 소망이 더디 이루어지면 그것이 마음을 상하게 하거니와 소원이 이루어지는 것은 곧 생명 나무니라 13 말씀을 멸시하는 자는 자기에게 패망을 이루고 계명을 두려워하는 자는 상을 받느니라 14 지혜 있는 자의 교훈은 생명의 샘이니 사망의 그물에서 벗어나게 하느니라 15 선한 지혜는 은혜를 베푸나 사악한 자의 길은 험하니라 16 무릇 슬기로운 자는 지식으로 행하거니와 미련한 자는 자기의 미련한 것을 나타내느니라 17 악한 사자는 재앙에 빠져도 충성된 사신은 양약이 되느니라 18 훈계를 저버리는 자에게는 궁핍과 수욕이 이르거니와 경계를 받는 자는 존영을 받느니라 19 소원을 성취하면 마음에 달아도 미련한 자는 악에서 떠나기를 싫어하느니라 20 지혜로운 자와 동행하면 지혜를 얻고 미련한 자와 사귀면 해를 받느니라 21 재앙은 죄인을 따르고 선한 보응은 의인에게 이르느니라

22 A good person leaves an inheritance for their children's children, but a sinner's wealth is stored up for the righteous.

23 An unplowed field produces food for the poor, but injustice sweeps it away.

24 Whoever spares the rod hates their children, but the one who loves their children is careful to discipline them.

25 The righteous eat to their hearts' content, but the stomach of the wicked goes hungry.

proverbs
14

1 The wise woman builds her house, but with her own hands the foolish one tears hers down.

2 Whoever fears the Lord walks uprightly, but those who despise him are devious in their ways.

3 A fool's mouth lashes out with pride, but the lips of the wise protect them.

4 Where there are no oxen, the manger is empty, but from the strength of an ox come abundant harvests.

5 An honest witness does not deceive, but a false witness pours out lies.

6 The mocker seeks wisdom and finds none, but knowledge comes easily to the discerning.

7 Stay away from a fool, for you will not find knowledge on their lips.

8 The wisdom of the prudent is to give thought to their ways, but the folly of fools is deception.

9 Fools mock at making amends for sin, but goodwill is found among the upright.

10 Each heart knows its own bitterness, and no one else can share its joy.

11 The house of the wicked will be destroyed, but the tent of the upright will flourish.

1 지혜로운 여인은 자기 집을 세우되 미련한 여인은 자기 손으로 그것을 허느니라 2 정직하게 행하는 자는 여호와를 경외하여도 패역하게 행하는 자는 여호와를 경멸하느니라 3 미련한 자는 교만하여 입으로 매를 자청하고 지혜로운 자의 입술은 자기를 보전하느니라 4 소가 없으면 구유는 깨끗하려니와 소의 힘으로 얻는 것이 많으니라 5 신실한 증인은 거짓말을 아니하여도 거짓 증인은 거짓말을 뱉느니라 6 거만한 자는 지혜를 구하여도 얻지 못하거니와 명철한 자는 지식 얻기가 쉬우니라 7 너는 미련한 자의 앞을 떠나라 그 입술에 지식 있음을 보지 못함이니라 8 슬기로운 자의 지혜는 자기의 길을 아는 것이라도 미련한 자의 어리석음은 속이는 것이니라 9 미련한 자는 죄를 심상히 여겨도 정직한 자 중에는 은혜가 있느니라 10 마음의 고통은 자기가 알고 마음의 즐거움은 타인이 참여하지 못하느니라 11 악한 자의 집은 망하겠고 정직한 자의 장막은 흥하리라

12 There is a way that appears to be right, but in the end it leads to death.

13 Even in laughter the heart may ache, and rejoicing may end in grief.

14 The faithless will be fully repaid for their ways, and the good rewarded for theirs.

15 The simple believe anything, but the prudent give thought to their steps.

16 The wise fear the Lord and shun evil, but a fool is hotheaded and yet feels secure.

17 A quick-tempered person does foolish things, and the one who devises evil schemes is hated.

18 The simple inherit folly, but the prudent are crowned with knowledge.

19 Evildoers will bow down in the presence of the good, and the wicked at the gates of the righteous.

20 The poor are shunned even by their neighbors, but the rich have many friends.

21 It is a sin to despise one's neighbor, but blessed is the one who is kind to the needy.

22 Do not those who plot evil go astray? But those who plan what is good find love and faithfulness.

23 All hard work brings a profit, but mere talk leads only to poverty.

12 어떤 길은 사람이 보기에 바르나 필경은 사망의 길이니라 13 웃을 때에도 마음에 슬픔이 있고 즐거움의 끝에도 근심이 있느니라 14 마음이 굽은 자는 자기 행위로 보응이 가득하겠고 선한 사람도 자기의 행위로 그러하리라 15 어리석은 자는 온갖 말을 믿으나 슬기로운 자는 자기의 행동을 삼가느니라 16 지혜로운 자는 두려워하여 악을 떠나나 어리석은 자는 방자하여 스스로 믿느니라 17 노하기를 속히 하는 자는 어리석은 일을 행하고 악한 계교를 꾀하는 자는 미움을 받느니라 18 어리석은 자는 어리석음으로 기업을 삼아도 슬기로운 자는 지식으로 면류관을 삼느니라 19 악인은 선인 앞에 엎드리고 불의한 자는 의인의 문에 엎드리느니라 20 가난한 자는 이웃에게도 미움을 받게 되나 부요한 자는 친구가 많으니라 21 이웃을 업신여기는 자는 죄를 범하는 자요 빈곤한 자를 불쌍히 여기는 자는 복이 있는 자니라 22 악을 도모하는 자는 잘못 가는 것이 아니냐 선을 도모하는 자에게는 인자와 진리가 있으리라 23 모든 수고에는 이익이 있어도 입술의 말은 궁핍을 이룰 뿐이니라

24 The wealth of the wise is their crown, but the folly of fools yields folly.

25 A truthful witness saves lives, but a false witness is deceitful.

26 Whoever fears the Lord has a secure fortress, and for their children it will be a refuge.

27 The fear of the Lord is a fountain of life, turning a person from the snares of death.

28 A large population is a king's glory, but without subjects a prince is ruined.

29 Whoever is patient has great understanding, but one who is quick-tempered displays folly.

30 A heart at peace gives life to the body, but envy rots the bones.

31 Whoever oppresses the poor shows contempt for their Maker, but whoever is kind to the needy honors God.

32 When calamity comes, the wicked are brought down, but even in death the righteous seek refuge in God.

33 Wisdom reposes in the heart of the discerning and even among fools she lets herself be known.

34 Righteousness exalts a nation, but sin condemns any people.

35 A king delights in a wise servant, but a shameful servant arouses his fury.

24 지혜로운 자의 재물은 그의 면류관이요 미련한 자의 소유는 다만 미련한 것이니라 25 진실한 증인은 사람의 생명을 구원하여도 거짓말을 뱉는 사람은 속이느니라 26 여호와를 경외하는 자에게는 견고한 의뢰가 있나니 그 자녀들에게 피난처가 있으리라 27 여호와를 경외하는 것은 생명의 샘이니 사망의 그물에서 벗어나게 하느니라 28 백성이 많은 것은 왕의 영광이요 백성이 적은 것은 주권자의 패망이니라 29 노하기를 더디 하는 자는 크게 명철하여도 마음이 조급한 자는 어리석음을 나타내느니라 30 평온한 마음은 육신의 생명이나 시기는 뼈를 썩게 하느니라 31 가난한 사람을 학대하는 자는 그를 지으신 이를 멸시하는 자요 궁핍한 사람을 불쌍히 여기는 자는 주를 공경하는 자니라 32 악인은 그의 환난에 엎드러져도 의인은 그의 죽음에도 소망이 있느니라 33 지혜는 명철한 자의 마음에 머물거니와 미련한 자의 속에 있는 것은 나타나느니라 34 공의는 나라를 영화롭게 하고 죄는 백성을 욕되게 하느니라 35 슬기롭게 행하는 신하는 왕에게 은총을 입고 욕을 끼치는 신하는 그의 진노를 당하느니라

1 A gentle answer turns away wrath, but a harsh word stirs up anger.

2 The tongue of the wise adorns knowledge, but the mouth of the fool gushes folly.

3 The eyes of the Lord are everywhere, keeping watch on the wicked and the good.

4 The soothing tongue is a tree of life, but a perverse tongue crushes the spirit.

5 A fool spurns a parent's discipline, but whoever heeds correction shows prudence.

6 The house of the righteous contains great treasure, but the income of the wicked brings ruin.

7 The lips of the wise spread knowledge, but the hearts of fools are not upright.

8 The Lord detests the sacrifice of the wicked, but the prayer of the upright pleases him.

9 The Lord detests the way of the wicked, but he loves those who pursue righteousness.

10 Stern discipline awaits anyone who leaves the path; the one who hates correction will die.

1 유순한 대답은 분노를 쉬게 하여도 과격한 말은 노를 격동하느니라 2 지혜 있는 자의 혀는 지식을 선히 베풀고 미련한 자의 입은 미련한 것을 쏟느니라 3 여호와의 눈은 어디서든지 악인과 선인을 감찰하시느니라 4 온순한 혀는 곧 생명 나무이지만 패역한 혀는 마음을 상하게 하느니라 5 아비의 훈계를 업신여기는 자는 미련한 자요 경계를 받는 자는 슬기를 얻을 자니라 6 의인의 집에는 많은 보물이 있어도 악인의 소득은 고통이 되느니라 7 지혜로운 자의 입술은 지식을 전파하여도 미련한 자의 마음은 정함이 없느니라 8 악인의 제사는 여호와께서 미워하셔도 정직한 자의 기도는 그가 기뻐하시느니라 9 악인의 길은 여호와께서 미워하셔도 공의를 따라가는 자는 그가 사랑하시느니라 10 도를 배반하는 자는 엄한 징계를 받을 것이요 견책을 싫어하는 자는 죽을 것이니라

11 Death and Destruction lie open before the Lord—how much more do human hearts!

12 Mockers resent correction, so they avoid the wise.

13 A happy heart makes the face cheerful, but heartache crushes the spirit.

14 The discerning heart seeks knowledge, but the mouth of a fool feeds on folly.

15 All the days of the oppressed are wretched, but the cheerful heart has a continual feast.

16 Better a little with the fear of the Lord than great wealth with turmoil.

17 Better a small serving of vegetables with love than a fattened calf with hatred.

18 A hot-tempered person stirs up conflict, but the one who is patient calms a quarrel.

19 The way of the sluggard is blocked with thorns, but the path of the upright is a highway.

20 A wise son brings joy to his father, but a foolish man despises his mother.

21 Folly brings joy to one who has no sense, but whoever has understanding keeps a straight course.

22 Plans fail for lack of counsel, but with many advisers they succeed.

11 스올과 아바돈도 여호와의 앞에 드러나거든 하물며 사람의 마음이리요 12 거만한 자는 견책 받기를 좋아하지 아니하며 지혜 있는 자에게로 가지도 아니하느니라 13 마음의 즐거움은 얼굴을 빛나게 하여도 마음의 근심은 심령을 상하게 하느니라 14 명철한 자의 마음은 지식을 요구하고 미련한 자의 입은 미련한 것을 즐기느니라 15 고난 받는 자는 그 날이 다 험악하나 마음이 즐거운 자는 항상 잔치하느니라 16 가산이 적어도 여호와를 경외하는 것이 크게 부하고 번뇌하는 것보다 나으니라 17 채소를 먹으며 서로 사랑하는 것이 살진 소를 먹으며 서로 미워하는 것보다 나으니라 18 분을 쉽게 내는 자는 다툼을 일으켜도 노하기를 더디 하는 자는 시비를 그치게 하느니라 19 게으른 자의 길은 가시 울타리 같으나 정직한 자의 길은 대로니라 20 지혜로운 아들은 아비를 즐겁게 하여도 미련한 자는 어미를 업신여기느니라 21 무지한 자는 미련한 것을 즐겨 하여도 명철한 자는 그 길을 바르게 하느니라 22 의논이 없으면 경영이 무너지고 지략이 많으면 경영이 성립하느니라

23 A person finds joy in giving an apt reply— and how good is a timely word!

24 The path of life leads upward for the prudent to keep them from going down to the realm of the dead.

25 The Lord tears down the house of the proud, but he sets the widow's boundary stones in place.

26 The Lord detests the thoughts of the wicked, but gracious words are pure in his sight.

27 The greedy bring ruin to their households, but the one who hates bribes will live.

28 The heart of the righteous weighs its answers, but the mouth of the wicked gushes evil.

29 The Lord is far from the wicked, but he hears the prayer of the righteous.

30 Light in a messenger's eyes brings joy to the heart, and good news gives health to the bones.

31 Whoever heeds life-giving correction will be at home among the wise.

32 Those who disregard discipline despise themselves, but the one who heeds correction gains understanding.

33 Wisdom's instruction is to fear the Lord, and humility comes before honor.

23 사람은 그 입의 대답으로 말미암아 기쁨을 얻나니 때에 맞는 말이 얼마나 아름다운고 24 지혜로운 자는 위로 향한 생명 길로 말미암음으로 그 아래에 있는 스올을 떠나게 되느니라 25 여호와는 교만한 자의 집을 허시며 과부의 지계를 정하시느니라 26 악한 꾀는 여호와께서 미워하시나 선한 말은 정결하니라 27 이익을 탐하는 자는 자기 집을 해롭게 하나 뇌물을 싫어하는 자는 살게 되느니라 28 의인의 마음은 대답할 말을 깊이 생각하여도 악인의 입은 악을 쏟느니라 29 여호와는 악인을 멀리 하시고 의인의 기도를 들으시느니라 30 눈이 밝은 것은 마음을 기쁘게 하고 좋은 기별은 뼈를 윤택하게 하느니라 31 생명의 경계를 듣는 귀는 지혜로운 자 가운데에 있느니라 32 훈계 받기를 싫어하는 자는 자기의 영혼을 경히 여김이라 견책을 달게 받는 자는 지식을 얻느니라 33 여호와를 경외하는 것은 지혜의 훈계라 겸손은 존귀의 길잡이니라

미리보는 어휘

PART

4

16-20

1 To humans belong the plans of the heart, but from the Lord comes the proper answer of the tongue.

2 All a person's ways seem pure to them, but motives are weighed by the Lord.

3 Commit to the Lord whatever you do, and he will establish your plans.

4 The Lord works out everything to its proper end— even the wicked for a day of disaster.

5 The Lord detests all the proud of heart. Be sure of this: They will not go unpunished.

6 Through love and faithfulness sin is atoned for; through the fear of the Lord evil is avoided.

7 When the Lord takes pleasure in anyone's way, he causes their enemies to make peace with them.

8 Better a little with righteousness than much gain with injustice.

9 In their hearts humans plan their course, but the Lord establishes their steps.

10 The lips of a king speak as an oracle, and his mouth does not betray justice.

1 마음의 경영은 사람에게 있어도 말의 응답은 여호와께로부터 나오느니라 2 사람의 행위가 자기 보기에는 모두 깨끗하여도 여호와는 심령을 감찰하시느니라 3 너의 행사를 여호와께 맡기라 그리하면 네가 경영하는 것이 이루어지리라 4 여호와께서 온갖 것을 그 쓰임에 적당하게 지으셨나니 악인도 악한 날에 적당하게 하셨느니라 5 무릇 마음이 교만한 자를 여호와께서 미워하시나니 피차 손을 잡을지라도 벌을 면하지 못하리라 6 인자와 진리로 인하여 죄악이 속하게 되고 여호와를 경외함으로 말미암아 악에서 떠나게 되느니라 7 사람의 행위가 여호와를 기쁘시게 하면 그 사람의 원수라도 그와 더불어 화목하게 하시느니라 8 적은 소득이 공의를 겸하면 많은 소득이 불의를 겸한 것보다 나으니라 9 사람이 마음으로 자기의 길을 계획할지라도 그의 걸음을 인도하시는 이는 여호와시니라 10 하나님의 말씀이 왕의 입술에 있은즉 재판할 때에 그의 입이 그르치지 아니하리라

11 Honest scales and balances belong to the Lord; all the weights in the bag are of his making.

12 Kings detest wrongdoing, for a throne is established through righteousness.

13 Kings take pleasure in honest lips; they value the one who speaks what is right.

14 A king's wrath is a messenger of death, but the wise will appease it.

15 When a king's face brightens, it means life; his favor is like a rain cloud in spring.

16 How much better to get wisdom than gold, to get insight rather than silver!

17 The highway of the upright avoids evil; those who guard their ways preserve their lives.

18 Pride goes before destruction, a haughty spirit before a fall.

19 Better to be lowly in spirit along with the oppressed than to share plunder with the proud.

20 Whoever gives heed to instruction prospers, and blessed is the one who trusts in the Lord.

21 The wise in heart are called discerning, and gracious words promote instruction.

22 Prudence is a fountain of life to the prudent, but folly brings punishment to fools.

11 공평한 저울과 접시 저울은 여호와의 것이요 주머니 속의 저울추도 다 그가 지으신 것이니라 12 악을 행하는 것은 왕들이 미워할 바니 이는 그 보좌가 공의로 말미암아 굳게 섬이니라 13 의로운 입술은 왕들이 기뻐하는 것이요 정직하게 말하는 자는 그들의 사랑을 입느니라 14 왕의 진노는 죽음의 사자들과 같아도 지혜로운 사람은 그것을 쉬게 하리라 15 왕의 희색은 생명을 뜻하나니 그의 은택이 늦은 비를 내리는 구름과 같으니라 16 지혜를 얻는 것이 금을 얻는 것보다 얼마나 나은고 명철을 얻는 것이 은을 얻는 것보다 더욱 나으니라 17 악을 떠나는 것은 정직한 사람의 대로이니 자기의 길을 지키는 자는 자기의 영혼을 보전하느니라 18 교만은 패망의 선봉이요 거만한 마음은 넘어짐의 앞잡이니라 19 겸손한 자와 함께 하여 마음을 낮추는 것이 교만한 자와 함께 하여 탈취물을 나누는 것보다 나으니라 20 삼가 말씀에 주의하는 자는 좋은 것을 얻나니 여호와를 의지하는 자는 복이 있느니라 21 마음이 지혜로운 자는 명철하다 일컬음을 받고 입이 선한 자는 남의 학식을 더하게 하느니라 22 명철한 자에게는 그 명철이 생명의 샘이 되거니와 미련한 자에게는 그 미련한 것이 징계가 되느니라

23 The hearts of the wise make their mouths prudent, and their lips promote instruction.

24 Gracious words are a honeycomb, sweet to the soul and healing to the bones.

25 There is a way that appears to be right, but in the end it leads to death.

26 The appetite of laborers works for them; their hunger drives them on.

27 A scoundrel plots evil, and on their lips it is like a scorching fire.

28 A perverse person stirs up conflict, and a gossip separates close friends.

29 A violent person entices their neighbor and leads them down a path that is not good.

30 Whoever winks with their eye is plotting perversity; whoever purses their lips is bent on evil.

31 Gray hair is a crown of splendor; it is attained in the way of righteousness.

32 Better a patient person than a warrior, one with self-control than one who takes a city.

33 The lot is cast into the lap, but its every decision is from the Lord.

1 Better a dry crust with peace and quiet than a house full of feasting, with strife.

2 A prudent servant will rule over a disgraceful son and will share the inheritance as one of the family.

3 The crucible for silver and the furnace for gold, but the Lord tests the heart.

4 A wicked person listens to deceitful lips; a liar pays attention to a destructive tongue.

5 Whoever mocks the poor shows contempt for their Maker; whoever gloats over disaster will not go unpunished.

6 Children's children are a crown to the aged, and parents are the pride of their children.

7 Eloquent lips are unsuited to a godless fool— how much worse lying lips to a ruler!

8 A bribe is seen as a charm by the one who gives it; they think success will come at every turn.

9 Whoever would foster love covers over an offense, but whoever repeats the matter separates close friends.

10 A rebuke impresses a discerning person more than a hundred lashes a fool.

1 마른 떡 한 조각만 있고도 화목하는 것이 제육이 집에 가득하고도 다투는 것보다 나으니라 2 슬기로운 종은 부끄러운 짓을 하는 주인의 아들을 다스리겠고 또 형제들 중에서 유업을 나누어 얻으리라 3 도가니는 은을, 풀무는 금을 연단하거니와 여호와는 마음을 연단하시느니라 4 악을 행하는 자는 사악한 입술이 하는 말을 잘 듣고 거짓말을 하는 자는 악한 혀가 하는 말에 귀를 기울이느니라 5 가난한 자를 조롱하는 자는 그를 지으신 주를 멸시하는 자요 사람의 재앙을 기뻐하는 자는 형벌을 면하지 못할 자니라 6 손자는 노인의 면류관이요 아비는 자식의 영화니라 7 지나친 말을 하는 것도 미련한 자에게 합당하지 아니하거든 하물며 거짓말을 하는 것이 존귀한 자에게 합당하겠느냐 8 뇌물은 그 임자가 보기에 보석 같은즉 그가 어디로 향하든지 형통하게 하느니라 9 허물을 덮어 주는 자는 사랑을 구하는 자요 그것을 거듭 말하는 자는 친한 벗을 이간하는 자니라 10 한 마디 말로 총명한 자에게 충고하는 것이 매 백 대로 미련한 자를 때리는 것보다 더욱 깊이 박히느니라

11 Evildoers foster rebellion against God; the messenger of death will be sent against them.

12 Better to meet a bear robbed of her cubs than a fool bent on folly.

13 Evil will never leave the house of one who pays back evil for good.

14 Starting a quarrel is like breaching a dam; so drop the matter before a dispute breaks out.

15 Acquitting the guilty and condemning the innocent— the Lord detests them both.

16 Why should fools have money in hand to buy wisdom, when they are not able to understand it?

17 A friend loves at all times, and a brother is born for a time of adversity.

18 One who has no sense shakes hands in pledge and puts up security for a neighbor.

19 Whoever loves a quarrel loves sin; whoever builds a high gate invites destruction.

20 One whose heart is corrupt does not prosper; one whose tongue is perverse falls into trouble.

21 To have a fool for a child brings grief; there is no joy for the parent of a godless fool.

22 A cheerful heart is good medicine, but a crushed spirit dries up the bones.

23 The wicked accept bribes in secret to pervert the course of justice.

24 A discerning person keeps wisdom in view, but a fool's eyes wander to the ends of the earth.

25 A foolish son brings grief to his father and bitterness to the mother who bore him.

26 If imposing a fine on the innocent is not good, surely to flog honest officials is not right.

27 The one who has knowledge uses words with restraint, and whoever has understanding is even-tempered.

28 Even fools are thought wise if they keep silent, and discerning if they hold their tongues.

1 An unfriendly person pursues selfish ends and against all sound judgment starts quarrels.

2 Fools find no pleasure in understanding but delight in airing their own opinions.

3 When wickedness comes, so does contempt, and with shame comes reproach.

4 The words of the mouth are deep waters, but the fountain of wisdom is a rushing stream.

5 It is not good to be partial to the wicked and so deprive the innocent of justice.

6 The lips of fools bring them strife, and their mouths invite a beating.

7 The mouths of fools are their undoing, and their lips are a snare to their very lives.

8 The words of a gossip are like choice morsels; they go down to the inmost parts.

9 One who is slack in his work is brother to one who destroys.

10 The name of the Lord is a fortified tower; the righteous run to it and are safe.

11 The wealth of the rich is their fortified city; they imagine it a wall too high to scale.

1 무리에게서 스스로 갈라지는 자는 자기 소욕을 따르는 자라 온갖 참 지혜를 배척하느니라 2 미련한 자는 명철을 기뻐하지 아니하고 자기의 의사를 드러내기만 기뻐하느니라 3 악한 자가 이를 때에는 멸시도 따라오고 부 끄러운 것이 이를 때에는 능욕도 함께 오느니라 4 명철한 사람의 입의 말은 깊은 물과 같고 지혜의 샘은 솟구쳐 흐르는 내와 같으니라 5 악인을 두둔하는 것과 재판할 때에 의인을 억울하게 하는 것이 선하지 아니하니라 6 미련한 자의 입술은 다툼을 일으키고 그의 입은 매를 자청하느니라 7 미련한 자의 입은 그의 멸망이 되고 그의 입술은 그의 영혼의 그물이 되느니라 8 남의 말하기를 좋아하는 자의 말은 별식과 같아서 뱃속 깊은 데로 내려가느니라 9 자기의 일을 게을리하는 자는 패가하는 자의 형제니라 10 여호와의 이름은 견고한 망대라 의인은 그리로 달려가서 안전함을 얻느니라 11 부자의 재물은 그의 견고한 성이라 그가 높은 성벽 같이 여기느니라

12 Before a downfall the heart is haughty, but humility comes before honor.

13 To answer before listening— that is folly and shame.

14 The human spirit can endure in sickness, but a crushed spirit who can bear?

15 The heart of the discerning acquires knowledge, for the ears of the wise seek it out.

16 A gift opens the way and ushers the giver into the presence of the great.

17 In a lawsuit the first to speak seems right, until someone comes forward and cross-examines.

18 Casting the lot settles disputes and keeps strong opponents apart.

19 A brother wronged is more unyielding than a fortified city; disputes are like the barred gates of a citadel.

20 From the fruit of their mouth a person's stomach is filled; with the harvest of their lips they are satisfied.

21 The tongue has the power of life and death, and those who love it will eat its fruit.

22 He who finds a wife finds what is good and receives favor from the Lord.

23 The poor plead for mercy, but the rich answer harshly.

24 One who has unreliable friends soon comes to ruin, but there is a friend who sticks closer than a brother.

12 사람의 마음의 교만은 멸망의 선봉이요 겸손은 존귀의 길잡이니라 13 사연을 듣기 전에 대답하는 자는 미련하여 욕을 당하느니라 14 사람의 심령은 그의 병을 능히 이기려니와 심령이 상하면 그것을 누가 일으키겠느냐 15 명철한 자의 마음은 지식을 얻고 지혜로운 자의 귀는 지식을 구하느니라 16 사람의 선물은 그의 길을 넓게 하며 또 존귀한 자 앞으로 그를 인도하느니라 17 송사에서는 먼저 온 사람의 말이 바른 것 같으나 그의 상대자가 와서 밝히느니라 18 제비 뽑는 것은 다툼을 그치게 하여 강한 자 사이에 해결하게 하느니라 19 노엽게 한 형제와 화목하기가 견고한 성을 취하기보다 어려운즉 이러한 다툼은 산성 문빗장 같으니라 20 사람은 입에서 나오는 열매로 말미암아 배부르게 되나니 곧 그의 입술에서 나는 것으로 말미암아 만족하게 되느니라 21 죽고 사는 것이 혀의 힘에 달렸나니 혀를 쓰기 좋아하는 자는 혀의 열매를 먹으리라 22 아내를 얻는 자는 복을 얻고 여호와께 은총을 받는 자니라 23 가난한 자는 간절한 말로 구하여도 부자는 엄한 말로 대답하느니라 24 많은 친구를 얻는 자는 해를 당하게 되거니와 어떤 친구는 형제보다 친밀하니라

1   Better the poor whose walk is blameless than a fool whose lips are perverse.

2   Desire without knowledge is not good— how much more will hasty feet miss the way!

3   A person's own folly leads to their ruin, yet their heart rages against the Lord.

4   Wealth attracts many friends, but even the closest friend of the poor person deserts them.

5   A false witness will not go unpunished, and whoever pours out lies will not go free.

6   Many curry favor with a ruler, and everyone is the friend of one who gives gifts.

7   The poor are shunned by all their relatives— how much more do their friends avoid them! Though the poor pursue them with pleading, they are nowhere to be found.

8   The one who gets wisdom loves life; the one who cherishes understanding will soon prosper.

9   A false witness will not go unpunished, and whoever pours out lies will perish.

10   It is not fitting for a fool to live in luxury— how much worse for a slave to rule over princes!

11 A person's wisdom yields patience; it is to one's glory to overlook an offense.

12 A king's rage is like the roar of a lion, but his favor is like dew on the grass.

13 A foolish child is a father's ruin, and a quarrelsome wife is like the constant dripping of a leaky roof.

14 Houses and wealth are inherited from parents, but a prudent wife is from the Lord.

15 Laziness brings on deep sleep, and the shiftless go hungry.

16 Whoever keeps commandments keeps their life, but whoever shows contempt for their ways will die.

17 Whoever is kind to the poor lends to the Lord, and he will reward them for what they have done.

18 Discipline your children, for in that there is hope; do not be a willing party to their death.

19 A hot-tempered person must pay the penalty; rescue them, and you will have to do it again.

20 Listen to advice and accept discipline, and at the end you will be counted among the wise.

21 Many are the plans in a person's heart, but it is the Lord's purpose that prevails.

11 노하기를 더디 하는 것이 사람의 슬기요 허물을 용서하는 것이 자기의 영광이니라 12 왕의 노함은 사자의 부르짖음 같고 그의 은택은 풀 위의 이슬 같으니라 13 미련한 아들은 그의 아비의 재앙이요 다투는 아내는 이어 떨어지는 물방울이니라 14 집과 재물 은 조상에게서 상속하거니와 슬기로운 아내는 여호와께로서 말미암느니라 15 게으름이 사람으로 깊이 잠들게 하나니 태만한 사 람은 주릴 것이니라 16 계명을 지키는 자는 자기의 영혼을 지키거니와 자기의 행실을 삼가지 아니하는 자는 죽으리라 17 가난한 자를 불쌍히 여기는 것은 여호와께 꾸어 드리는 것이니 그의 선행을 그에게 갚아 주시리라 18 네가 네 아들에게 희망이 있은즉 그 를 징계하되 죽일 마음은 두지 말지니라 19 노하기를 맹렬히 하는 자는 벌을 받을 것이라 네가 그를 건져 주면 다시 그런 일이 생기 리라 20 너는 권고를 들으며 훈계를 받으라 그리하면 네가 필경은 지혜롭게 되리라 21 사람의 마음에는 많은 계획이 있어도 오직 여호와의 뜻만이 완전히 서리라

22 What a person desires is unfailing love; better to be poor than a liar.

23 The fear of the Lord leads to life; then one rests content, untouched by trouble.

24 A sluggard buries his hand in the dish; he will not even bring it back to his mouth!

25 Flog a mocker, and the simple will learn prudence; rebuke the discerning, and they will gain knowledge.

26 Whoever robs their father and drives out their mother is a child who brings shame and disgrace.

27 Stop listening to instruction, my son, and you will stray from the words of knowledge.

28 A corrupt witness mocks at justice, and the mouth of the wicked gulps down evil.

29 Penalties are prepared for mockers, and beatings for the backs of fools.

1 Wine is a mocker and beer a brawler; whoever is led astray by them is not wise.

2 A king's wrath strikes terror like the roar of a lion; those who anger him forfeit their lives.

3 It is to one's honor to avoid strife, but every fool is quick to quarrel.

4 Sluggards do not plow in season; so at harvest time they look but find nothing.

5 The purposes of a person's heart are deep waters, but one who has insight draws them out.

6 Many claim to have unfailing love, but a faithful person who can find?

7 The righteous lead blameless lives; blessed are their children after them.

8 When a king sits on his throne to judge, he winnows out all evil with his eyes.

9 Who can say, "I have kept my heart pure; I am clean and without sin"?

10 Differing weights and differing measures— the Lord detests them both.

11 Even small children are known by their actions, so is their conduct really pure and upright?

12 Ears that hear and eyes that see— the Lord has made them both.

13 Do not love sleep or you will grow poor; stay awake and you will have food to spare.

14 "It's no good, it's no good!" says the buyer— then goes off and boasts about the purchase.

15 Gold there is, and rubies in abundance, but lips that speak knowledge are a rare jewel.

16 Take the garment of one who puts up security for a stranger; hold it in pledge if it is done for an outsider.

17 Food gained by fraud tastes sweet, but one ends up with a mouth full of gravel.

18 Plans are established by seeking advice; so if you wage war, obtain guidance.

19 A gossip betrays a confidence; so avoid anyone who talks too much.

20 If someone curses their father or mother, their lamp will be snuffed out in pitch darkness.

21 An inheritance claimed too soon will not be blessed at the end.

22 Do not say, "I'll pay you back for this wrong!" Wait for the LORD, and he will avenge you.

23 The Lord detests differing weights, and dishonest scales do not please him.

24 A person's steps are directed by the Lord. How then can anyone understand their own way?

25 It is a trap to dedicate something rashly and only later to consider one's vows.

26 A wise king winnows out the wicked; he drives the threshing wheel over them.

27 The human spirit is the lamp of the Lord that sheds light on one's inmost being.

28 Love and faithfulness keep a king safe; through love his throne is made secure.

29 The glory of young men is their strength, gray hair the splendor of the old.

30 Blows and wounds scrub away evil, and beatings purge the inmost being.

미리보는 어휘

PART

5

21–25

1 In the Lord's hand the king's heart is a stream of water that he channels toward all who please him.

2 A person may think their own ways are right, but the Lord weighs the heart.

3 To do what is right and just is more acceptable to the Lord than sacrifice.

4 Haughty eyes and a proud heart— the unplowed field of the wicked—produce sin.

5 The plans of the diligent lead to profit as surely as haste leads to poverty.

6 A fortune made by a lying tongue is a fleeting vapor and a deadly snare.

7 The violence of the wicked will drag them away, for they refuse to do what is right.

8 The way of the guilty is devious, but the conduct of the innocent is upright.

9 Better to live on a corner of the roof than share a house with a quarrelsome wife.

10 The wicked crave evil; their neighbors get no mercy from them.

1 왕의 마음이 여호와의 손에 있음이 마치 봇물과 같아서 그가 임의로 인도하시느니라   2 사람의 행위가 자기 보기에는 모두 정직하여도 여호와는 마음을 감찰하시느니라   3 공의와 정의를 행하는 것은 제사 드리는 것보다 여호와께서 기쁘게 여기시느니라   4 눈이 높은 것과 마음이 교만한 것과 악인이 형통한 것은 다 죄니라   5 부지런한 자의 경영은 풍부함에 이를 것이나 조급한 자는 궁핍함에 이를 따름이니라   6 속이는 말로 재물을 모으는 것은 죽음을 구하는 것이라 곧 불려다니는 안개니라   7 악인의 강포는 자기를 소멸하나니 이는 정의를 행하기 싫어함이니라   8 죄를 크게 범한 자의 길은 심히 구부러지고 깨끗한 자의 길은 곧으니라   9 다투는 여인과 함께 큰 집에서 사는 것보다 움막에서 사는 것이 나으니라   10 악인의 마음은 남의 재앙을 원하나니 그 이웃도 그 앞에서 은혜를 입지 못하느니라

11 When a mocker is punished, the simple gain wisdom; by paying attention to the wise they get knowledge.

12 The Righteous One takes note of the house of the wicked and brings the wicked to ruin.

13 Whoever shuts their ears to the cry of the poor will also cry out and not be answered.

14 A gift given in secret soothes anger, and a bribe concealed in the cloak pacifies great wrath.

15 When justice is done, it brings joy to the righteous but terror to evildoers.

16 Whoever strays from the path of prudence comes to rest in the company of the dead.

17 Whoever loves pleasure will become poor; whoever loves wine and olive oil will never be rich.

18 The wicked become a ransom for the righteous, and the unfaithful for the upright.

19 Better to live in a desert than with a quarrelsome and nagging wife.

20 The wise store up choice food and olive oil, but fools gulp theirs down.

21 Whoever pursues righteousness and love finds life, prosperity and honor.

22 One who is wise can go up against the city of the mighty and pull down the stronghold in which they trust.

23 Those who guard their mouths and their tongues keep themselves from calamity.

24 The proud and arrogant person—"Mocker" is his name— behaves with insolent fury.

25 The craving of a sluggard will be the death of him, because his hands refuse to work.

26 All day long he craves for more, but the righteous give without sparing.

27 The sacrifice of the wicked is detestable— how much more so when brought with evil intent!

28 A false witness will perish, but a careful listener will testify successfully.

29 The wicked put up a bold front, but the upright give thought to their ways.

30 There is no wisdom, no insight, no plan that can succeed against the Lord.

31 The horse is made ready for the day of battle, but victory rests with the Lord.

22 지혜로운 자는 용사의 성에 올라가서 그 성이 의지하는 방벽을 허느니라 23 입과 혀를 지키는 자는 자기의 영혼을 환난에서 보전하느니라 24 무례하고 교만한 자를 이름하여 망령된 자라 하나니 이는 넘치는 교만으로 행함이니라 25 게으른 자의 욕망이 자기를 죽이나니 이는 자기의 손으로 일하기를 싫어함이니라 26 어떤 자는 종일토록 탐하기만 하나 의인은 아끼지 아니하고 베푸느니라 27 악인의 제물은 본래 가증하거든 하물며 악한 뜻으로 드리는 것이랴 28 거짓 증인은 패망하려니와 확실히 들은 사람의 말은 힘이 있느니라 29 악인은 자기의 얼굴을 굳게 하나 정직한 자는 자기의 행위를 삼가느니라 30 지혜로도 못하고, 명철로도 못하고 모략으로도 여호와를 당하지 못하느니라 31 싸울 날을 위하여 마병을 예비하거니와 이김은 여호와께 있느니라

1 A good name is more desirable than great riches; to be esteemed is better than silver or gold.

2 Rich and poor have this in common: The Lord is the Maker of them all.

3 The prudent see danger and take refuge, but the simple keep going and pay the penalty.

4 Humility is the fear of the Lord; its wages are riches and honor and life.

5 In the paths of the wicked are snares and pitfalls, but those who would preserve their life stay far from them.

6 Start children off on the way they should go, and even when they are old they will not turn from it.

7 The rich rule over the poor, and the borrower is slave to the lender.

8 Whoever sows injustice reaps calamity, and the rod they wield in fury will be broken.

9 The generous will themselves be blessed, for they share their food with the poor.

10 Drive out the mocker, and out goes strife; quarrels and insults are ended.

1 많은 재물보다 명예를 택할 것이요 은이나 금보다 은총을 더욱 택할 것이니라 2 가난한 자와 부한 자가 함께 살거니와 그 모두를 지으신 이는 여호와시니라 3 슬기로운 자는 재앙을 보면 숨어 피하여도 어리석은 자는 나가다가 해를 받느니라 4 겸손과 여호와를 경외함의 보상은 재물과 영광과 생명이니라 5 패역한 자의 길에는 가시와 올무가 있거니와 영혼을 지키는 자는 이를 멀리 하느니라 6 마땅히 행할 길을 아이에게 가르치라 그리하면 늙어도 그것을 떠나지 아니하리라 7 부자는 가난한 자를 주관하고 빚진 자는 채주의 종이 되느니라 8 악을 뿌리는 자는 재앙을 거두리니 그 분노의 기세가 쇠하리라 9 선한 눈을 가진 자는 복을 받으리니 이는 양식을 가난한 자에게 줌이니라 10 거만한 자를 쫓아내면 다툼이 쉬고 싸움과 수욕이 그치느니라

11 One who loves a pure heart and who speaks with grace will have the king for a friend.

12 The eyes of the Lord keep watch over knowledge, but he frustrates the words of the unfaithful.

13 The sluggard says, "There's a lion outside! I'll be killed in the public square!"

14 The mouth of an adulterous woman is a deep pit; a man who is under the Lord's wrath falls into it.

15 Folly is bound up in the heart of a child, but the rod of discipline will drive it far away.

16 One who oppresses the poor to increase his wealth and one who gives gifts to the rich—both come to poverty.

Sayings of the Wise

17 Pay attention and turn your ear to the sayings of the wise; apply your heart to what I teach,

18 for it is pleasing when you keep them in your heart and have all of them ready on your lips.

19 So that your trust may be in the Lord, I teach you today, even you.

20 Have I not written thirty sayings for you, sayings of counsel and knowledge,

11 마음의 정결을 사모하는 자의 입술에는 덕이 있으므로 임금이 그의 친구가 되느니라 12 여호와의 눈은 지식 있는 사람을 지키시나 사악한 사람의 말은 패하게 하시느니라 13 게으른 자는 말하기를 사자가 밖에 있은즉 내가 나가면 거리에서 찢기겠다 하느니라 14 음녀의 입은 깊은 함정이라 여호와의 노를 당한 자는 거기 빠지리라 15 아이의 마음에는 미련한 것이 얽혔으나 징계하는 채찍이 이를 멀리 쫓아내리라 16 이익을 얻으려고 가난한 자를 학대하는 자와 부자에게 주는 자는 가난하여질 뿐이니라 17 너는 귀를 기울여 지혜 있는 자의 말씀을 들으며 내 지식에 마음을 둘지어다 18 이것을 네 속에 보존하며 네 입술 위에 함께 있게 함이 아름다우니라 19 내가 네게 여호와를 의뢰하게 하려 하여 이것을 오늘 특별히 네게 알게 하였노니 20 내가 모략과 지식의 아름다운 것을 너를 위해 기록하여

21 teaching you to be honest and to speak the truth, so that you bring back truthful reports to those you serve?

22 Do not exploit the poor because they are poor and do not crush the needy in court,

23 for the Lord will take up their case and will exact life for life.

24 Do not make friends with a hot-tempered person, do not associate with one easily angered,

25 or you may learn their ways and get yourself ensnared.

26 Do not be one who shakes hands in pledge or puts up security for debts;

27 if you lack the means to pay, your very bed will be snatched from under you.

28 Do not move an ancient boundary stone set up by your ancestors.

29 Do you see someone skilled in their work? They will serve before kings; they will not serve before officials of low rank.

1 When you sit to dine with a ruler, note well what is before you,

2 and put a knife to your throat if you are given to gluttony.

3 Do not crave his delicacies, for that food is deceptive.

4 Do not wear yourself out to get rich; do not trust your own cleverness.

5 Cast but a glance at riches, and they are gone, for they will surely sprout wings and fly off to the sky like an eagle.

6 Do not eat the food of a begrudging host, do not crave his delicacies;

7 for he is the kind of person who is always thinking about the cost. "Eat and drink," he says to you, but his heart is not with you.

8 You will vomit up the little you have eaten and will have wasted your compliments.

9 Do not speak to fools, for they will scorn your prudent words.

10 Do not move an ancient boundary stone or encroach on the fields of the fatherless,

11 for their Defender is strong; he will take up their case against you.

12 Apply your heart to instruction and your ears to words of knowledge.

1 네가 관원과 함께 앉아 음식을 먹게 되거든 삼가 네 앞에 있는 자가 누구인지를 생각하며 2 네가 만일 음식을 탐하는 자이거든 네 목에 칼을 둘 것이니라 3 그의 맛있는 음식을 탐하지 말라 그것은 속이는 음식이니라 4 부자 되기에 애쓰지 말고 네 사사로운 지혜를 버릴지어다 5 네가 어찌 허무한 것에 주목하겠느냐 정녕히 재물은 스스로 날개를 내어 하늘을 나는 독수리처럼 날아가리라 6 악한 눈이 있는 자의 음식을 먹지 말며 그의 맛있는 음식을 탐하지 말지어다 7 대저 그 마음의 생각이 어떠하면 그 위인도 그러한즉 그가 네게 먹고 마시라 할지라도 그의 마음은 너와 함께 하지 아니함이라 8 네가 조금 먹은 것도 토하겠고 네 아름다운 말도 헛된 데로 돌아가리라 9 미련한 자의 귀에 말하지 말지니 이는 그가 네 지혜로운 말을 업신여길 것임이니라 10 옛 지계석을 옮기지 말며 고아들의 밭을 침범하지 말지어다 11 대저 그들의 구속자는 강하시니 그가 너를 대적하여 그들의 원한을 풀어 주시리라 12 훈계에 착심하며 지식의 말씀에 귀를 기울이라

13 Do not withhold discipline from a child; if you punish them with the rod, they will not die.

14 Punish them with the rod and save them from death.

15 My son, if your heart is wise, then my heart will be glad indeed;

16 my inmost being will rejoice when your lips speak what is right.

17 Do not let your heart envy sinners, but always be zealous for the fear of the Lord.

18 There is surely a future hope for you, and your hope will not be cut off.

19 Listen, my son, and be wise, and set your heart on the right path:

20 Do not join those who drink too much wine or gorge themselves on meat,

21 for drunkards and gluttons become poor, and drowsiness clothes them in rags.

22 Listen to your father, who gave you life, and do not despise your mother when she is old.

23 Buy the truth and do not sell it— wisdom, instruction and insight as well.

24 The father of a righteous child has great joy; a man who fathers a wise son rejoices in him.

---

13 아이를 훈계하지 아니하려고 하지 말라 채찍으로 그를 때릴지라도 그가 죽지 아니하리라 14 네가 그를 채찍으로 때리면 그의 영혼을 스올에서 구원하리라 15 내 아들아 만일 네 마음이 지혜로우면 나 곧 내 마음이 즐겁겠고 16 만일 네 입술이 정직을 말하면 내 속이 유쾌하리라 17 네 마음으로 죄인의 형통을 부러워하지 말고 항상 여호와를 경외하라 18 정녕히 네 장래가 있겠고 네 소망이 끊어지지 아니하리라 19 내 아들아 너는 듣고 지혜를 얻어 네 마음을 바른 길로 인도할지니라 20 술을 즐겨 하는 자들과 고기를 탐하는 자들과도 더불어 사귀지 말라 21 술 취하고 음식을 탐하는 자는 가난하여질 것이요 잠 자기를 즐겨 하는 자는 해어진 옷을 입을 것임이니라 22 너를 낳은 아비에게 청종하고 네 늙은 어미를 경히 여기지 말지니라 23 진리를 사되 팔지는 말며 지혜와 훈계와 명철도 그리할지니라 24 의인의 아비는 크게 즐거울 것이요 지혜로운 자식을 낳은 자는 그로 말미암아 즐거울 것이니라

25 May your father and mother rejoice; may she who gave you birth be joyful!

26 My son, give me your heart and let your eyes delight in my ways,

27 for an adulterous woman is a deep pit, and a wayward wife is a narrow well.

28 Like a bandit she lies in wait and multiplies the unfaithful among men.

29 Who has woe? Who has sorrow? Who has strife? Who has complaints? Who has needless bruises? Who has bloodshot eyes?

30 Those who linger over wine, who go to sample bowls of mixed wine.

31 Do not gaze at wine when it is red, when it sparkles in the cup, when it goes down smoothly!

32 In the end it bites like a snake and poisons like a viper.

33 Your eyes will see strange sights, and your mind will imagine confusing things.

34 You will be like one sleeping on the high seas, lying on top of the rigging.

35 "They hit me," you will say, "but I'm not hurt! They beat me, but I don't feel it! When will I wake up so I can find another drink?"

25 네 부모를 즐겁게 하며 너를 낳은 어미를 기쁘게 하라 26 내 아들아 네 마음을 내게 주며 네 눈으로 내 길을 즐거워할지어다 27 대저 음녀는 깊은 구덩이요 이방 여인은 좁은 함정이라 28 참으로 그는 강도 같이 매복하며 사람들 중에 사악한 자가 많아지게 하느니라 29 재앙이 뉘게 있느뇨 근심이 뉘게 있느뇨 분쟁이 뉘게 있느뇨 원망이 뉘게 있느뇨 까닭 없는 상처가 뉘게 있느뇨 붉은 눈이 뉘게 있느뇨 30 술에 잠긴 자에게 있고 혼합한 술을 구하러 다니는 자에게 있느니라 31 포도주는 붉고 잔에서 번쩍이며 순하게 내려가나니 너는 그것을 보지도 말지어다 32 그것이 마침내 뱀 같이 물 것이요 독사 같이 쏠 것이며 33 또 네 눈에는 괴이한 것이 보일 것이요 네 마음은 구부러진 말을 할 것이며 34 너는 바다 가운데에 누운 자 같을 것이요 돛대 위에 누운 자 같을 것이며 35 네가 스스로 말하기를 사람이 나를 때려도 나는 아프지 아니하고 나를 상하게 하여도 내게 감각이 없다 내가 언제나 깰까 다시 술을 찾겠다 하리라

1 Do not envy the wicked, do not desire their company;

2 for their hearts plot violence, and their lips talk about making trouble.

3 By wisdom a house is built, and through understanding it is established;

4 through knowledge its rooms are filled with rare and beautiful treasures.

5 The wise prevail through great power, and those who have knowledge muster their strength.

6 Surely you need guidance to wage war, and victory is won through many advisers.

7 Wisdom is too high for fools; in the assembly at the gate they must not open their mouths.

8 Whoever plots evil will be known as a schemer.

9 The schemes of folly are sin, and people detest a mocker.

10 If you falter in a time of trouble, how small is your strength!

11 Rescue those being led away to death; hold back those staggering toward slaughter.

1 너는 악인의 형통함을 부러워하지 말며 그와 함께 있으려고 하지도 말지어다 2 그들의 마음은 강포를 품고 그들의 입술은 재앙을 말함이니라 3 집은 지혜로 말미암아 건축되고 명철로 말미암아 견고하게 되며 4 또 방들은 지식으로 말미암아 각종 귀하고 아름다운 보배로 채우게 되느니라 5 지혜 있는 자는 강하고 지식 있는 자는 힘을 더하나니 6 너는 전략으로 싸우라 승리는 지략이 많음에 있느니라 7 지혜는 너무 높아서 미련한 자가 미치지 못할 것이므로 그는 성문에서 입을 열지 못하느니라 8 악행하기를 꾀하는 자를 일컬어 사악한 자라 하느니라 9 미련한 자의 생각은 죄요 거만한 자는 사람에게 미움을 받느니라 10 네가 만일 환난 날에 낙담하면 네 힘이 미약함을 보임이니라 11 너는 사망으로 끌려가는 자를 건져 주며 살륙을 당하게 된 자를 구원하지 아니하려고 하지 말라

12 If you say, "But we knew nothing about this," does not he who weighs the heart perceive it? Does not he who guards your life know it? Will he not repay everyone according to what they have done?

13 Eat honey, my son, for it is good; honey from the comb is sweet to your taste.

14 Know also that wisdom is like honey for you: If you find it, there is a future hope for you, and your hope will not be cut off.

15 Do not lurk like a thief near the house of the righteous, do not plunder their dwelling place;

16 for though the righteous fall seven times, they rise again, but the wicked stumble when calamity strikes.

17 Do not gloat when your enemy falls; when they stumble, do not let your heart rejoice,

18 or the Lord will see and disapprove and turn his wrath away from them.

19 Do not fret because of evildoers or be envious of the wicked,

20 for the evildoer has no future hope, and the lamp of the wicked will be snuffed out.

21 Fear the Lord and the king, my son, and do not join with rebellious officials,

22 for those two will send sudden destruction on them, and who knows what calamities they can bring?

23 These also are sayings of the wise: To show partiality in judging is not good:

24 Whoever says to the guilty, "You are innocent," will be cursed by peoples and denounced by nations.

25 But it will go well with those who convict the guilty, and rich blessing will come on them.

26 An honest answer is like a kiss on the lips.

27 Put your outdoor work in order and get your fields ready; after that, build your house.

28 Do not testify against your neighbor without cause— would you use your lips to mislead?

29 Do not say, "I'll do to them as they have done to me; I'll pay them back for what they did."

30 I went past the field of a sluggard, past the vineyard of someone who has no sense;

31 thorns had come up everywhere, the ground was covered with weeds, and the stone wall was in ruins.

32 I applied my heart to what I observed and learned a lesson from what I saw:

33 A little sleep, a little slumber, a little folding of the hands to rest—

34 and poverty will come on you like a thief and scarcity like an armed man.

More Proverbs of Solomon

1 These are more proverbs of Solomon, compiled by the men of Hezekiah king of Judah:

2 It is the glory of God to conceal a matter; to search out a matter is the glory of kings.

3 As the heavens are high and the earth is deep, so the hearts of kings are unsearchable.

4 Remove the dross from the silver, and a silversmith can produce a vessel;

5 remove wicked officials from the king's presence, and his throne will be established through righteousness.

6 Do not exalt yourself in the king's presence, and do not claim a place among his great men;

7 it is better for him to say to you, "Come up here," than for him to humiliate you before his nobles. What you have seen with your eyes

8 do not bring hastily to court, for what will you do in the end if your neighbor puts you to shame?

9 If you take your neighbor to court, do not betray another's confidence,

1 이것도 솔로몬의 잠언이요 유다 왕 히스기야의 신하들이 편집한 것이니라 2 일을 숨기는 것은 하나님의 영화요 일을 살피는 것은 왕의 영화니라 3 하늘의 높음과 땅의 깊음 같이 왕의 마음은 헤아릴 수 없느니라 4 은에서 찌꺼기를 제하라 그리하면 장색의 쓸 만한 그릇이 나올 것이요 5 왕 앞에서 악한 자를 제하라 그리하면 그의 왕위가 의로 말미암아 견고히 서리라 6 왕 앞에서 스스로 높은 체하지 말며 대인들의 자리에 서지 말라 7 이는 사람이 네게 이리로 올라오라고 말하는 것이 네 눈에 보이는 귀인 앞에서 저리로 내려가라고 말하는 것보다 나음이니라 8 너는 서둘러 나가서 다투지 말라 마침내 네가 이웃에게서 욕을 보게 될 때에 네가 어찌할 줄을 알지 못할까 두려우니라 9 너는 이웃과 다투거든 변론만 하고 남의 은밀한 일은 누설하지 말라

10 or the one who hears it may shame you and the charge against you will stand.

11 Like apples of gold in settings of silver is a ruling rightly given.

12 Like an earring of gold or an ornament of fine gold is the rebuke of a wise judge to a listening ear.

13 Like a snow-cooled drink at harvest time is a trustworthy messenger to the one who sends him; he refreshes the spirit of his master.

14 Like clouds and wind without rain is one who boasts of gifts never given.

15 Through patience a ruler can be persuaded, and a gentle tongue can break a bone.

16 If you find honey, eat just enough— too much of it, and you will vomit.

17 Seldom set foot in your neighbor's house— too much of you, and they will hate you.

18 Like a club or a sword or a sharp arrow is one who gives false testimony against a neighbor.

19 Like a broken tooth or a lame foot is reliance on the unfaithful in a time of trouble.

20 Like one who takes away a garment on a cold day, or like vinegar poured on a wound, is one who sings songs to a heavy heart.heart.

10 듣는 자가 너를 꾸짖을 터이요 또 네게 대한 악평이 네게서 떠나지 아니할까 두려우니라 11 경우에 합당한 말은 아로새긴 은 쟁반에 금 사과니라 12 슬기로운 자의 책망은 청종하는 귀에 금 고리와 정금 장식이니라 13 충성된 사자는 그를 보낸 이에게 마치 추수하는 날에 얼음 냉수 같아서 능히 그 주인의 마음을 시원하게 하느니라 14 선물한다고 거짓 자랑하는 자는 비 없는 구름과 바람 같으니라 15 오래 참으면 관원도 설득할 수 있나니 부드러운 혀는 뼈를 꺾느니라 16 너는 꿀을 보거든 족하리만큼 먹으라 과식함으로 토할까 두려우니라 17 너는 이웃집에 자주 다니지 말라 그가 너를 싫어하며 미워할까 두려우니라 18 자기의 이웃을 쳐서 거짓 증거하는 사람은 방망이요 칼이요 뾰족한 화살이니라 19 환난 날에 진실하지 못한 자를 의뢰하는 것은 부러진 이와 위골된 발 같으니라 20 마음이 상한 자에게 노래하는 것은 추운 날에 옷을 벗음 같고 소다 위에 식초를 부음 같으니라

21 If your enemy is hungry, give him food to eat; if he is thirsty, give him water to drink.

22 In doing this, you will heap burning coals on his head, and the Lord will reward you.

23 Like a north wind that brings unexpected rain is a sly tongue— which provokes a horrified look.

24 Better to live on a corner of the roof than share a house with a quarrelsome wife.

25 Like cold water to a weary soul is good news from a distant land.

26 Like a muddied spring or a polluted well are the righteous who give way to the wicked.

27 It is not good to eat too much honey, nor is it honorable to search out matters that are too deep.

28 Like a city whose walls are broken through is a person who lacks self-control.

26장

abomination 가증한 행위
flutter 날개치다
archer 궁사
deception 속임
discreetly 신중하게
ember 깜부기불
rod 매, 회초리
fervent 열정적인
firebrand 횃불
swallow 제비
limp 기운이 없는
morsel 특히 맛있는
thornbush 가시나무
flattering 아첨하는
halter 고삐
undeserved 부당한
meddle in : 간섭하다, 참견하다

27장

boast 자랑하다
contempt 멸시
crucible 도가니
incense 향
nourish ⋯에게 먹을 것을 주다
loathe 싫어하다
overwhelm 압도하다
provocation 화남, 분개
prudent 신중한, 현명한
restrain 제어하다
wound 상처, 부상
mortar 절구
furnace 풀무
pestle 절굿공이
spring from... : ⋯로부터 솟아나오다
hold...in pledge : ⋯를 저당잡다

28장

amass 축적하다
discernment 분별
elation 의기양양
exorbitant 과대한
glutton 폭식하는 사람
perverse 뒤틀어진, 잘못된
rebellious 반역하는
dissension 불화
fugitive 도망자
greedy 탐욕스러운
ill-gotten 부정하게 얻은
partiality 편파
prosper 번영하다
remedy 치유책
renounce 폐기하다
thrive 번성하다
torment 괴롭히다
be eager to... : ⋯을 열망하다

29장

prostitute 창녀
squander 탕진하다
stiff-necked 완고한
accomplice 공범
audience 접견
bloodthirsty 잔인한
correction 징계
haste 서두름
impart 주다, 가르치다
integrity 성실, 완전
oppressor 억압자
pamper 오냐오냐하다
rage 분노하다
revelation 계시
scoff 비웃다
testify 증언하다
stir up : 소란케 하다

30장

barren 불임의
disdainful 경멸하는
filth 더러운 것
flawless 흠없는
hollow 음푹한 곳
leech 거머리
shield 방패
slander 중상하다
churn 휘젓다
displace 대신 들어서다
lizard 도마뱀
locust 메뚜기
raven 갈까마귀
stately 당당한
stride 발걸음
strut 활보하다
peck out : 쪼아먹다
exalt oneself : 잘난척하다

31장

vigor 정력, 힘
anguish 고뇌
crave 탐하다
deprive 빼앗다, 허용치 않다
dignity 위엄
distaff 실톳대, 실패
idleness 게으름
sash 장식띠
spindle 물렛가락
vigorously 힘있게
deceptive 속이는
fleeting 덧없는, 순식간의
speak up for... : …를 위해 변호하다
take one's seat : 자리잡다

proverbs
26

1 Like snow in summer or rain in harvest, honor is not fitting for a fool.

2 Like a fluttering sparrow or a darting swallow, an undeserved curse does not come to rest.

3 A whip for the horse, a bridle for the donkey, and a rod for the backs of fools!

4 Do not answer a fool according to his folly, or you yourself will be just like him.

5 Answer a fool according to his folly, or he will be wise in his own eyes.

6 Sending a message by the hands of a fool is like cutting off one's feet or drinking poison.

7 Like the useless legs of one who is lame is a proverb in the mouth of a fool.

8 Like tying a stone in a sling is the giving of honor to a fool.

9 Like a thornbush in a drunkard's hand is a proverb in the mouth of a fool.

10 Like an archer who wounds at random is one who hires a fool or any passer-by.

11 As a dog returns to its vomit, so fools repeat their folly.

12 Do you see a person wise in their own eyes? There is more hope for a fool than for them.

13 A sluggard says, "There's a lion in the road, a fierce lion roaming the streets!"

14 As a door turns on its hinges, so a sluggard turns on his bed.

15 A sluggard buries his hand in the dish; he is too lazy to bring it back to his mouth.

16 A sluggard is wiser in his own eyes than seven people who answer discreetly.

17 Like one who grabs a stray dog by the ears is someone who rushes into a quarrel not their own.

18 Like a maniac shooting flaming arrows of death

19 is one who deceives their neighbor and says, "I was only joking!"

20 Without wood a fire goes out; without a gossip a quarrel dies down.

21 As charcoal to embers and as wood to fire, so is a quarrelsome person for kindling strife.

22 The words of a gossip are like choice morsels; they go down to the inmost parts.

23 Like a coating of silver dross on earthenware are fervent lips with an evil heart.

24 Enemies disguise themselves with their lips, but in their hearts they harbor deceit.

25 Though their speech is charming, do not believe them, for seven abominations fill their hearts.

26 Their malice may be concealed by deception, but their wickedness will be exposed in the assembly.

27 Whoever digs a pit will fall into it; if someone rolls a stone, it will roll back on them.

28 A lying tongue hates those it hurts, and a flattering mouth works ruin.

1 Do not boast about tomorrow, for you do not know what a day may bring.

2 Let someone else praise you, and not your own mouth; an outsider, and not your own lips.

3 Stone is heavy and sand a burden, but a fool's provocation is heavier than both.

4 Anger is cruel and fury overwhelming, but who can stand before jealousy?

5 Better is open rebuke than hidden love.

6 Wounds from a friend can be trusted, but an enemy multiplies kisses.

7 One who is full loathes honey from the comb, but to the hungry even what is bitter tastes sweet.

8 Like a bird that flees its nest is anyone who flees from home.

9 Perfume and incense bring joy to the heart, and the pleasantness of a friend springs from their heartfelt advice.

10 Do not forsake your friend or a friend of your family, and do not go to your relative's house when disaster strikes you— better a neighbor nearby than a relative far away.

1 너는 내일 일을 자랑하지 말라 하루 동안에 무슨 일이 일어날는지 네가 알 수 없음이니라 2 타인이 너를 칭찬하게 하고 네 입으로는 하지 말며 외인이 너를 칭찬하게 하고 네 입술로는 하지 말지니라 3 돌은 무겁고 모래도 가볍지 아니하거니와 미련한 자의 분노는 이 둘보다 무거우니라 4 분은 잔인하고 노는 창수 같거니와 투기 앞에야 누가 서리요 5 면책은 숨은 사랑보다 나으니라 6 친구의 아픈 책망은 충직으로 말미암는 것이나 원수의 잦은 입맞춤은 거짓에서 난 것이니라 7 배부른 자는 꿀이라도 싫어하고 주린 자에게는 쓴 것이라도 다니라 8 고향을 떠나 유리하는 사람은 보금자리를 떠나 떠도는 새와 같으니라 9 기름과 향이 사람의 마음을 즐겁게 하나니 친구의 충성된 권고가 이와 같이 아름다우니라 10 네 친구와 네 아비의 친구를 버리지 말며 네 환난 날에 형제의 집에 들어가지 말지어다 가까운 이웃이 먼 형제보다 나으니라

11 Be wise, my son, and bring joy to my heart; then I can answer anyone who treats me with contempt.

12 The prudent see danger and take refuge, but the simple keep going and pay the penalty.

13 Take the garment of one who puts up security for a stranger; hold it in pledge if it is done for an outsider.

14 If anyone loudly blesses their neighbor early in the morning, it will be taken as a curse.

15 A quarrelsome wife is like the dripping of a leaky roof in a rainstorm;

16 restraining her is like restraining the wind or grasping oil with the hand.

17 As iron sharpens iron, so one person sharpens another.

18 The one who guards a fig tree will eat its fruit, and whoever protects their master will be honored.

19 As water reflects the face, so one's life reflects the heart.

20 Death and Destruction are never satisfied, and neither are human eyes.

21 The crucible for silver and the furnace for gold, but people are tested by their praise.

11 내 아들아 지혜를 얻고 내 마음을 기쁘게 하라 그리하면 나를 비방하는 자에게 내가 대답할 수 있으리라 12 슬기로운 자는 재앙을 보면 숨어 피하여도 어리석은 자들은 나가다가 해를 받느니라 13 타인을 위하여 보증 선 자의 옷을 취하라 외인들을 위하여 보증 선 자는 그의 몸을 볼모 잡을지니라 14 이른 아침에 큰 소리로 자기 이웃을 축복하면 도리어 저주 같이 여기게 되리라 15 다투는 여자는 비 오는 날에 이어 떨어지는 물방울이라 16 그를 제어하기가 바람을 제어하는 것 같고 오른손으로 기름을 움키는 것 같으니라 17 철이 철을 날카롭게 하는 것 같이 사람이 그의 친구의 얼굴을 빛나게 하느니라 18 무화과나무를 지키는 자는 그 과실을 먹고 자기 주인에게 시중드는 자는 영화를 얻느니라 19 물에 비치면 얼굴이 서로 같은 것 같이 사람의 마음도 서로 비치느니라 20 스올과 아바돈은 만족함이 없고 사람의 눈도 만족함이 없느니라 21 도가니로 은을, 풀무로 금을, 칭찬으로 사람을 단련하느니라

22 Though you grind a fool in a mortar, grinding them like grain with a pestle, you will not remove their folly from them.

23 Be sure you know the condition of your flocks, give careful attention to your herds;

24 for riches do not endure forever, and a crown is not secure for all generations.

25 When the hay is removed and new growth appears and the grass from the hills is gathered in,

26 the lambs will provide you with clothing, and the goats with the price of a field.

27 You will have plenty of goats' milk to feed your family and to nourish your female servants.

22 미련한 자를 곡물과 함께 절구에 넣고 공이로 찧을지라도 그의 미련은 벗겨지지 아니하느니라 23 네 양 떼의 형편을 부지런히 살피며 네 소 떼에게 마음을 두라 24 대저 재물은 영원히 있지 못하나니 면류관이 어찌 대대에 있으랴 25 풀을 벤 후에는 새로 움이 돋나니 산에서 꼴을 거둘 것이니라 26 어린 양의 털은 네 옷이 되며 염소는 밭을 사는 값이 되며 27 염소의 젖은 넉넉하여 너와 네 집의 음식이 되며 네 여종의 먹을 것이 되느니라

proverbs
28

1 The wicked flee though no one pursues, but the righteous are as bold as a lion.

2 When a country is rebellious, it has many rulers, but a ruler with discernment and knowledge maintains order.

3 A ruler who oppresses the poor is like a driving rain that leaves no crops.

4 Those who forsake instruction praise the wicked, but those who heed it resist them.

5 Evildoers do not understand what is right, but those who seek the Lord understand it fully.

6 Better the poor whose walk is blameless than the rich whose ways are perverse.

7 A discerning son heeds instruction, but a companion of gluttons disgraces his father.

8 Whoever increases wealth by taking interest or profit from the poor amasses it for another, who will be kind to the poor.

9 If anyone turns a deaf ear to my instruction, even their prayers are detestable.

10 Whoever leads the upright along an evil path will fall into their own trap, but the blameless will receive a good inheritance.

11 The rich are wise in their own eyes; one who is poor and discerning sees how deluded they are.

12 When the righteous triumph, there is great elation; but when the wicked rise to power, people go into hiding.

13 Whoever conceals their sins does not prosper, but the one who confesses and renounces them finds mercy.

14 Blessed is the one who always trembles before God, but whoever hardens their heart falls into trouble.

15 Like a roaring lion or a charging bear is a wicked ruler over a helpless people.

16 A tyrannical ruler practices extortion, but one who hates ill-gotten gain will enjoy a long reign.

17 Anyone tormented by the guilt of murder will seek refuge in the grave; let no one hold them back.

18 The one whose walk is blameless is kept safe, but the one whose ways are perverse will fall into the pit.

19 Those who work their land will have abundant food, but those who chase fantasies will have their fill of poverty.

20 A faithful person will be richly blessed, but one eager to get rich will not go unpunished.

21 To show partiality is not good— yet a person will do wrong for a piece of bread.

22 The stingy are eager to get rich and are unaware that poverty awaits them.

23 Whoever rebukes a person will in the end gain favor rather than one who has a flattering tongue.

24 Whoever robs their father or mother and says, "It's not wrong," is partner to one who destroys.

25 The greedy stir up conflict, but those who trust in the Lord will prosper.

26 Those who trust in themselves are fools, but those who walk in wisdom are kept safe.

27 Those who give to the poor will lack nothing, but those who close their eyes to them receive many curses.

28 When the wicked rise to power, people go into hiding; but when the wicked perish, the righteous thrive.

22 악한 눈이 있는 자는 재물을 얻기에만 급하고 빈궁이 자기에게로 임할 줄은 알지 못하느니라 23 사람을 경책하는 자는 혀로 아첨하는 자보다 나중에 더욱 사랑을 받느니라 24 부모의 물건을 도둑질하고서도 죄가 아니라 하는 자는 멸망 받게 하는 자의 동류니라 25 욕심이 많은 자는 다툼을 일으키나 여호와를 의지하는 자는 풍족하게 되느니라 26 자기의 마음을 믿는 자는 미련한 자요 지혜롭게 행하는 자는 구원을 얻을 자니라 27 가난한 자를 구제하는 자는 궁핍하지 아니하려니와 못 본 체하는 자에게는 저주가 크리라 28 악인이 일어나면 사람이 숨고 그가 멸망하면 의인이 많아지느니라

1 Whoever remains stiff-necked after many rebukes will suddenly be destroyed—without remedy.

2 When the righteous thrive, the people rejoice; when the wicked rule, the people groan.

3 A man who loves wisdom brings joy to his father, but a companion of prostitutes squanders his wealth.

4 By justice a king gives a country stability, but those who are greedy for bribes tear it down.

5 Those who flatter their neighbors are spreading nets for their feet.

6 Evildoers are snared by their own sin, but the righteous shout for joy and are glad.

7 The righteous care about justice for the poor, but the wicked have no such concern.

8 Mockers stir up a city, but the wise turn away anger.

9 If a wise person goes to court with a fool, the fool rages and scoffs, and there is no peace.

10 The bloodthirsty hate a person of integrity and seek to kill the upright.

1 자주 책망을 받으면서도 목이 곧은 사람은 갑자기 패망을 당하고 피하지 못하리라 2 의인이 많아지면 백성이 즐거워하고 악인이 권세를 잡으면 백성이 탄식하느니라 3 지혜를 사모하는 자는 아비를 즐겁게 하여도 창기와 사귀는 자는 재물을 잃느니라 4 왕은 정의로 나라를 견고하게 하나 뇌물을 억지로 내게 하는 자는 나라를 멸망시키느니라 5 이웃에게 아첨하는 것은 그의 발 앞에 그물을 치는 것이니라 6 악인이 범죄하는 것은 스스로 올무가 되게 하는 것이나 의인은 노래하고 기뻐하느니라 7 의인은 가난한 자의 사정을 알아 주나 악인은 알아 줄 지식이 없느니라 8 거만한 자는 성읍을 요란하게 하여도 슬기로운 자는 노를 그치게 하느니라 9 지혜로운 자와 미련한 자가 다투면 지혜로운 자가 노하든지 웃든지 그 다툼은 그침이 없느니라 10 피 흘리기를 좋아하는 자는 온전한 자를 미워하고 정직한 자의 생명을 찾느니라

11 Fools give full vent to their rage, but the wise bring calm in the end.

12 If a ruler listens to lies, all his officials become wicked.

13 The poor and the oppressor have this in common: The Lord gives sight to the eyes of both.

14 If a king judges the poor with fairness, his throne will be established forever.

15 A rod and a reprimand impart wisdom, but a child left undisciplined disgraces its mother.

16 When the wicked thrive, so does sin, but the righteous will see their downfall.

17 Discipline your children, and they will give you peace; they will bring you the delights you desire.

18 Where there is no revelation, people cast off restraint; but blessed is the one who heeds wisdom's instruction.

19 Servants cannot be corrected by mere words; though they understand, they will not respond.

20 Do you see someone who speaks in haste? There is more hope for a fool than for them.

21 A servant pampered from youth will turn out to be insolent.

22 An angry person stirs up conflict, and a hot-tempered person commits many sins.

23 Pride brings a person low, but the lowly in spirit gain honor.

24 The accomplices of thieves are their own enemies; they are put under oath and dare not testify.

25 Fear of man will prove to be a snare, but whoever trusts in the Lord is kept safe.

26 Many seek an audience with a ruler, but it is from the Lord that one gets justice.

27 The righteous detest the dishonest; the wicked detest the upright.

22 노하는 자는 다툼을 일으키고 성내는 자는 범죄함이 많으니라 23 사람이 교만하면 낮아지게 되겠고 마음이 겸손하면 영예를 얻으리라 24 도둑과 짝하는 자는 자기의 영혼을 미워하는 자라 그는 저주를 들어도 진술하지 아니하느니라 25 사람을 두려워하면 올무에 걸리게 되거니와 여호와를 의지하는 자는 안전하리라 26 주권자에게 은혜를 구하는 자가 많으나 사람의 일의 작정은 여호와께로 말미암느니라 27 불의한 자는 의인에게 미움을 받고 바르게 행하는 자는 악인에게 미움을 받느니라

proverbs

30

Sayings of Agur

1   The sayings of Agur son of Jakeh—an inspired utterance. This man's utterance to Ithiel: "I am weary, God, but I can prevail.

2   Surely I am only a brute, not a man; I do not have human understanding.

3   I have not learned wisdom, nor have I attained to the knowledge of the Holy One.

4   Who has gone up to heaven and come down? Whose hands have gathered up the wind? Who has wrapped up the waters in a cloak? Who has established all the ends of the earth? What is his name, and what is the name of his son? Surely you know!

5   "Every word of God is flawless; he is a shield to those who take refuge in him.

6   Do not add to his words, or he will rebuke you and prove you a liar.

7   "Two things I ask of you, Lord; do not refuse me before I die:

8   Keep falsehood and lies far from me; give me neither poverty nor riches, but give me only my daily bread.

9   Otherwise, I may have too much and disown you and say, 'Who is the Lord?' Or I may become poor and steal, and so dishonor the name of my God.

1 이 말씀은 야게의 아들 아굴의 잠언이니 그가 이디엘 곧 이디엘과 우갈에게 이른 것이니라 2 나는 다른 사람에게 비하면 짐승이라 내게는 사람의 총명이 있지 아니하니라 3 나는 지혜를 배우지 못하였고 또 거룩하신 자를 아는 지식이 없거니와 4 하늘에 올라 갔다가 내려온 자가 누구인지, 바람을 그 장중에 모은 자가 누구인지, 물을 옷에 싼 자가 누구인지, 땅의 모든 끝을 정한 자가 누구인지, 그의 이름이 무엇인지, 그의 아들의 이름이 무엇인지 너는 아느냐 5 하나님의 말씀은 다 순전하며 하나님은 그를 의지하는 자의 방패시니라 6 너는 그의 말씀에 더하지 말라 그가 너를 책망하시겠고 너는 거짓말하는 자가 될까 두려우니라 7 내가 두 가지 일을 주께 구하였사오니 내가 죽기 전에 내게 거절하지 마시옵소서 8 곧 헛된 것과 거짓말을 내게서 멀리 하옵시며 나를 가난하게도 마옵시고 부하게도 마옵시고 오직 필요한 양식으로 나를 먹이시옵소서 9 혹 내가 배불러서 하나님을 모른다 여호와가 누구냐 할까 하오며 혹 내가 가난하여 도둑질하고 내 하나님의 이름을 욕되게 할까 두려워함이니이다

10 "Do not slander a servant to their master, or they will curse you, and you will pay for it.

11 "There are those who curse their fathers and do not bless their mothers;

12 those who are pure in their own eyes and yet are not cleansed of their filth;

13 those whose eyes are ever so haughty, whose glances are so disdainful;

14 those whose teeth are swords and whose jaws are set with knives to devour the poor from the earth and the needy from among mankind.

15 "The leech has two daughters. 'Give! Give!' they cry. "There are three things that are never satisfied, four that never say, 'Enough!':

16 the grave, the barren womb, land, which is never satisfied with water, and fire, which never says, 'Enough!'

17 "The eye that mocks a father, that scorns an aged mother, will be pecked out by the ravens of the valley, will be eaten by the vultures.

18 "There are three things that are too amazing for me, four that I do not understand:

19 the way of an eagle in the sky, the way of a snake on a rock, the way of a ship on the high seas, and the way of a man with a young woman.

20 "This is the way of an adulterous woman: She eats and wipes her mouth and says, 'I've done nothing wrong.'

21 "Under three things the earth trembles, under four it cannot bear up:

22 a servant who becomes king, a godless fool who gets plenty to eat,

23 a contemptible woman who gets married, and a servant who displaces her mistress.

24 "Four things on earth are small, yet they are extremely wise:

25 Ants are creatures of little strength, yet they store up their food in the summer;

26 hyraxes are creatures of little power, yet they make their home in the crags;

27 locusts have no king, yet they advance together in ranks;

28 a lizard can be caught with the hand, yet it is found in kings' palaces.

29 "There are three things that are stately in their stride, four that move with stately bearing:

30 a lion, mighty among beasts, who retreats before nothing;

31 a strutting rooster, a he-goat, and a king secure against revolt.

32 "If you play the fool and exalt yourself, or if you plan evil, clap your hand over your mouth!

33 For as churning cream produces butter, and as twisting the nose produces blood, so stirring up anger produces strife."

Sayings of King Lemuel

1 The sayings of King Lemuel—an inspired utterance his mother taught him.

2 Listen, my son! Listen, son of my womb! Listen, my son, the answer to my prayers!

3 Do not spend your strength on women, your vigor on those who ruin kings.

4 It is not for kings, Lemuel— it is not for kings to drink wine, not for rulers to crave beer,

5 lest they drink and forget what has been decreed, and deprive all the oppressed of their rights.

6 Let beer be for those who are perishing, wine for those who are in anguish!

7 Let them drink and forget their poverty and remember their misery no more.

8 Speak up for those who cannot speak for themselves, for the rights of all who are destitute.

9 Speak up and judge fairly; defend the rights of the poor and needy.

1 르무엘 왕이 말씀한 바 곧 그의 어머니가 그를 훈계한 잠언이라 2 내 아들아 내가 무엇을 말하랴 내 태에서 난 아들아 내가 무엇을 말하랴 서원대로 얻은 아들아 내가 무엇을 말하랴 3 네 힘을 여자들에게 쓰지 말며 왕들을 멸망시키는 일을 행하지 말지어다 4 르무엘아 포도주를 마시는 것이 왕들에게 마땅하지 아니하고 왕들에게 마땅하지 아니하며 독주를 찾는 것이 주권자들에게 마땅하지 않도다 5 술을 마시다가 법을 잊어버리고 모든 곤고한 자들의 송사를 굽게 할까 두려우니라 6 독주는 죽게 된 자에게, 포도주는 마음에 근심하는 자에게 줄지어다 7 그는 마시고 자기의 빈궁한 것을 잊어버리겠고 다시 자기의 고통을 기억하지 아니하리라 8 너는 말 못하는 자와 모든 고독한 자의 송사를 위하여 입을 열지니라 9 너는 입을 열어 공의로 재판하여 곤고한 자와 궁핍한 자를 신원할지니라

10 A wife of noble character who can find? She is worth far more than rubies.

11 Her husband has full confidence in her and lacks nothing of value.

12 She brings him good, not harm, all the days of her life.

13 She selects wool and flax and works with eager hands.

14 She is like the merchant ships, bringing her food from afar.

15 She gets up while it is still night; she provides food for her family and portions for her female servants.

16 She considers a field and buys it; out of her earnings she plants a vineyard.

17 She sets about her work vigorously; her arms are strong for her tasks.

18 She sees that her trading is profitable, and her lamp does not go out at night.

19 In her hand she holds the distaff and grasps the spindle with her fingers.

20 She opens her arms to the poor and extends her hands to the needy.

21 When it snows, she has no fear for her household; for all of them are clothed in scarlet.

10 누가 현숙한 여인을 찾아 얻겠느냐 그의 값은 진주보다 더 하니라 11 그런 자의 남편의 마음은 그를 믿나니 산업이 핍절하지 아니하겠으며 12 그런 자는 살아 있는 동안에 그의 남편에게 선을 행하고 악을 행하지 아니하느니라 13 그는 양털과 삼을 구하여 부지런히 손으로 일하며 14 상인의 배와 같아서 먼 데서 양식을 가져 오며 15 밤이 새기 전에 일어나서 자기 집안 사람들에게 음식을 나누어 주며 여종들에게 일을 정하여 맡기며 16 밭을 살펴 보고 사며 자기의 손으로 번 것을 가지고 포도원을 일구며 17 힘 있게 허리를 묶으며 자기의 팔을 강하게 하며 18 자기의 장사가 잘 되는 줄을 깨닫고 밤에 등불을 끄지 아니하며 19 손으로 솜뭉치를 들고 손가락으로 가락을 잡으며 20 그는 곤고한 자에게 손을 펴며 궁핍한 자를 위하여 손을 내밀며 21 자기 집 사람들은 다 홍색 옷을 입었으므로 눈이 와도 그는 자기 집 사람들을 위하여 염려하지 아니하며

22 She makes coverings for her bed; she is clothed in fine linen and purple.

23 Her husband is respected at the city gate, where he takes his seat among the elders of the land.

24 She makes linen garments and sells them, and supplies the merchants with sashes.

25 She is clothed with strength and dignity; she can laugh at the days to come.

26 She speaks with wisdom, and faithful instruction is on her tongue.

27 She watches over the affairs of her household and does not eat the bread of idleness.

28 Her children arise and call her blessed; her husband also, and he praises her:

29 "Many women do noble things, but you surpass them all."

30 Charm is deceptive, and beauty is fleeting; but a woman who fears the Lord is to be praised.

31 Honor her for all that her hands have done, and let her works bring her praise at the city gate.

22 그는 자기를 위하여 아름다운 이불을 지으며 세마포와 자색 옷을 입으며 23 그의 남편은 그 땅의 장로들과 함께 성문에 앉으며 사람들의 인정을 받으며 24 그는 베로 옷을 지어 팔며 띠를 만들어 상인들에게 맡기며 25 능력과 존귀로 옷을 삼고 후일을 웃으며 26 입을 열어 지혜를 베풀며 그의 혀로 인애의 법을 말하며 27 자기의 집안 일을 보살피고 게을리 얻은 양식을 먹지 아니하나니 28 그의 자식들은 일어나 감사하며 그의 남편은 칭찬하기를 29 덕행 있는 여자가 많으나 그대는 모든 여자보다 뛰어나다 하느니라 30 고운 것도 거짓되고 아름다운 것도 헛되나 오직 여호와를 경외하는 여자는 칭찬을 받을 것이라 31 그 손의 열매가 그에게로 돌아갈 것이요 그 행한 일로 말미암아 성문에서 칭찬을 받으리라

Trust in the LORD with all your heart
and lean not on your own understanding;

in all your ways acknowledge him,
and he will make your paths straight.

Proverbs 3:5-6

영어성경
잠언 필사를 마치며...

영어성경 쓰다시리즈 - ❶
|
영어성경 잠언.쓰다
PROVERBS WRITE

펴낸곳	에이프릴지저스
엮은이	에이프릴지저스 편집부

등록번호	제2019-000161호
주소	경기도 고양시 일산서구 주화로180
전화	031-908-3432 팩스 0504-230-0965
이메일	apriljesus2017@gmail.com

I S B N   979-11-90850-18-6 04230,
I S B N   979-11-90850-17-9 04230(set)
값은 뒤표지에 있습니다. 잘못된 책은 바꿔 드립니다.

홈페이지	www.apriljesus.com
인스타그램	instagram.com/apriljesus

Ⓐ 에이프릴지저스